NEW LONGMAN LITERATURE

Literary Non-fiction Collection

PEARSON

Longman

Edinburgh Gate
Harlow, Essex

Pearson Education Limited
Edinburgh Gate
Harlow
Essex
CM20 2JE
England

This educational edition first published by Pearson Education 2005

ISBN 1405 80666 4

Printed in China

The Publisher's policy is to use paper manufactured from sustainable forests.

Volume Editor: Alastair West
Contributors: Helen Lines and Cindy Torn

We are grateful to the following for permission to reproduce photographs:

Action Plus: (Neil Tingle); **Ardea:** (Francois Gohier); **TopFoto:** (Branger/Roger Viollet):

Picture research by Sandra Hilsdon

Contents

Science

Good science writing can make you see aspects of the familiar world around you in a new light. Scientists observe, experiment, measure and set out laws to describe and explain how the world is. For example, why is it that some mammals live in the sea rather than on land? How will global warming affect us? Why is Santa so fat? One of the challenges for science writers is to make facts and difficult explanations accessible for ordinary, non-specialist readers. The best science writers can enable us all to share the excitement of scientific discovery and help us to reflect on the significance of what they describe. The scientists writing in this section work in very different fields but they are all able to convey why science is so important in our lives. As you read these extracts, think about how these writers bring alive facts, statistics and technical information in a way that you can enjoy and understand.

Return to the water

Sir David Attenborough

How do whales communicate across such vast distances and depths in the oceans? Do whales live and behave in a similar way to land mammals? In this extract from his book The Life of Mammals, *which accompanied a BBC TV series with the same title, Sir David Attenborough describes how whales communicate and reflects on the similarity between the behaviour of some whales and that of a pride of lions. As you read:*
- *think about what Attenborough finds amazing about the whale and how he conveys this sense of wonder to you.*

The blue whale is the biggest animal of any kind that has ever existed on earth. The largest of the dinosaurs is thought to have weighed around 100 tons. The blue whale can grow to lengths of 110 feet and weights of 190 tons. It is not surprising that a sea-living creature should exceed the weight of any terrestrial animal for bone is simply not strong enough a material to carry such immense weights. In the sea, however, water supports an animal's body and bones do no more than provide its framework.

The whale's body is streamlined to perfection. It is entirely shrouded by a blanket of blubber which in places is twenty inches thick. Its forelegs have become slender flippers. Its hind legs have disappeared altogether except for small **relict bones**[1] within its flanks. It has no external ears and no external genitals.

Until very recently, blue whales were among the most **elusive**[2] animals in the sea. They are solitary and cruise at up to twenty knots on unpredictable courses through the immensities of the open ocean, so encountering one was largely a matter of luck. But now scientists have perfected techniques that can take observers to within a few yards of these immense animals. Painstaking observations have begun to reveal their traditional migration routes. A slow-flying aircraft circling several hundred feet up for hours at a time over likely stretches of ocean will with luck be able to spot one in the clear blue seas even though it is fully submerged. Radio calls from the air to a fast launch can direct it to roughly the right patch of water. Once there, a fast rubber dinghy can leave the launch and head at speed towards a distant spout as the animal surfaces to breathe. A skilled helmsman, knowledgeable about whale behaviour, can then judge where the cruising whale may next come up to breathe and take you there.

You look over the side and if you are lucky, the sapphire blue of the Pacific water will begin to pale. You realise that something flat, horizontal and vast is slowly rising from the depths towards the surface. It's the whale's tail. You look ahead, seventy feet, almost the length of a tennis court, and a grey hump breaks the surface with the waves

---

[1] **relict bones**: bones which have survived evolution, even though they are no longer of use
[2] **elusive**: difficult to find

3

swilling over it. It is so far away that it hardly seems possible for it to be connected to the flat white shape still rising beside your dinghy. A pair of nostrils opens in the distant hump and with a whoosh, a plume of vapour blasts thirty feet into the sky. Fishy-smelling droplets of mucus may fleck your face. The whale is **idling**[1]. Even so it is sliding through the water so swiftly the dinghy can barely keep up with it. The whale's head may rise and spout a few more times but then the tail breaks the surface and rears up into the air, dripping with water. It is as wide as the wings of a small aircraft. The next dive the whale makes will be a deep one. It may be gone for an hour and you can have little idea of where it will have travelled to in that time. Your encounter is over.

The blue whale, the biggest of all animals, lives on some of the smallest – krill, small shrimp-like **crustaceans**[2] a couple of inches long. It captures them, millions at a time, by opening its jaws and **distending**[3] its pleated throat so that its mouth fills with water. It then half shuts its jaws and expels the water by pushing forward its gargantuan fleshy tongue. A blue whale's tongue is as big as an elephant. This forces the water out of its mouth through a line of bristle-fringed horny slats, the baleen, that hang from the whale's toothless upper jaw. The krill is left behind to be swept off the baleen by the tongue and then swallowed.

No environment on land can parallel the conditions in

---

[1] **idling**: moving lazily without direction

[2] **crustaceans**: sea creatures with shells

[3] **distending**: expanding

which these mammals live. They move freely in three dimensions. Uninterrupted water may stretch horizontally around them for hundreds of miles. Below them it reaches downwards for maybe a mile or more into inky blackness. In such watery emptiness, how do these mammals navigate around the globe to find their food or one another? They probably have a reasonable sense of taste that enables them to savour the faint traces of chemical ingredients that might distinguish different parts of the ocean, but that is likely to be of only limited value in feeding or reacting with one another.

They have eyes, but these are very small and can be of little use under most circumstances for even in clear water it is not possible to see great distances and at depth, of course, eyes are no use at all.

But they can hear. Whales do not have external ears and the opening of the ear canal, even in the biggest whales, is tiny, no more than a centimetre in diameter. But their hearing, nonetheless, is acute. Sound travels further and faster in water than it does in air. A loud noise in the sea can be heard without undue distortion hundreds of miles away. So they must be able to pick up the distant thunder of the waves breaking on the shore, the high pitched snaps and twitterings of crustaceans, the sound of marine engines and revolving propellers. It now seems that they can navigate by **sonar***, as bats do, but on a vastly greater

---

* **sonar**: a way of using sound waves to locate objects and judge distances underwater

5

scale. A blue whale travelling through the North Atlantic seemed to be bouncing its calls off the continental shelf of Northern Ireland. But, above all, they can hear one another.

Baleen whales, in particular the humpback, a smaller cousin of the blue whale, exploit sound to the full in organising their social life. During the breeding season, the males hang in mid-water producing long sequences of sounds – deep moans, whoops, soaring **glissandi**[1], high squeaks and **staccato**[2] grunts. Several humpbacked whales, separated from one another by miles of water, may be singing at the same time. What is more, all those in the same population will be singing the same phrases in the same sequences. But each individual makes his own decision as to how many times he repeats each component phrase before he moves to the next sequence. A complete song may last for ten minutes and a whale may repeat it continuously for twenty-four hours at a time. It seems that female humpbacks, like female birds, use these songs as a basis for selecting their mates. ...

Mammals first took to water to find food. There was plenty of it there – fish, molluscs, crustaceans, plants. But today there is a greater variety than ever before. Now there are other mammals. Grey whales are 40 foot long filter-feeders. Every spring those in the eastern Pacific assemble in the warm shallow lagoons of Baja California

---

[1] **glissandi**: runs of musical notes
[2] **staccato**: short and sharp

off the coast of Mexico. Here the females give birth to their calves. In the spring, they begin a long journey up the western coasts of north America to the Arctic where they will feed on the **burgeoning*** numbers of shrimps, worms and other invertebrates that swarm in the sediment of the sea floor. The males and non-breeding females lead the way, travelling at around four knots. The journey north is six thousand miles long. The young whales cannot tackle it until they are several months old, so the last to leave are the females with young. They will be travelling slowly for a calf can only swim half as fast as an adult. Off the coast of California, pods of killer whales lie in wait for them.

Killer whales are normally very vocal but when they detect the approach of a grey whale and her calf they fall silent. They start to follow the pair. Before long the whale and her calf become aware that they are being chased. The mother increases her speed, encouraging her calf to swim as fast as it can, but the killers have no difficulty in keeping up. They take turns in harassing the calf. They have to be careful, for the female could severely injure them with a blow from her tail. After three or four hours, the calf is so exhausted that it can go no further. The killers force themselves between it and the mother. Once it is separated, the killers swim over it, forcing it downwards, preventing it from breathing. Eventually, the calf drowns and the killers make their meal. Often all they eat is the tongue. The rest of the body is left to sink slowly to the sea floor.

---

* **burgeoning**: rapidly growing

The parallel between such killer whales and the packs of lions preying on wildebeest and their calves as they migrate across the African savannahs is an obvious one. Mammals have become so at home in the sea that now the ancient duels that they have fought between themselves for so long on land are being continued, even in the remote waters of the open oceans.

Gluttony: Santa's genetics

Roger Highfield

The science journalist, Roger Highfield, writes a weekly column on science in the Daily Telegraph. *Each year in December he tries to give a seasonal, humorous flavour to his article. In this piece he reminds us of the traditional image of the paunchy, jolly Father Christmas figure. Clearly a weight problem here! Perhaps so much overeating every Christmas makes him like this. Or is there another explanation? What can modern science tell us about this case? As you read:*

- *think about how the writer uses humour to make his explanation accessible.*

Think of the way Santa is usually depicted on Christmas cards. One obvious aspect of his appearance attracts little comment. Not his white beard, ruddy complexion or tendency to 'Ho-ho-ho' at any opportunity. Nor the company he keeps: the reindeer, snowmen and his diminutive helpers. I am thinking of another Santa **trait***, one that – amazingly for our image-conscious society – is not often discussed. It is that huge stomach.

Generations of children have asked how Santa manages to squeeze down chimneys. But few, if any, have asked the most obvious question of all: why is Santa so fat? After all,

---

*****trait**: characteristic

if he lost a few pounds, surely his job would be that much easier? Santa would then also provide an influential model of moderation, restraint and self-control during the festivities. Perhaps Santa's rolls of flesh and overwhelming cheerfulness are the result of seasonal excesses. Perhaps his girth is the result of eating the millions of mince pies left out for him on Christmas Eve.

But what if the jolly, fat Santa is more than just a cliché? What follows is, I admit, speculative. However, recent advances in genetic science suggest that Father Christmas may have a **defective**[1] gene. Because this gene has been disrupted by a 'spelling error' in his DNA, Santa has a propensity to pile on the pounds. There is even evidence that he may also suffer from **diabetes**[2].

Santa is not alone. Obesity is now the most common nutritional disorder in the Western world. In America, for example, one-third of adults are overweight. The incidence of obesity – defined as weighing 20 per cent or more above the maximum desirable body weight – is rising particularly fast in children. Since 1976, prevalence of **paediatric obesity**[3] has increased by more than 50 per cent. Eight in ten obese adolescents grow up to be obese adults.

In Britain, one-third of the population carry too much fat and about 5 per cent are actually obese. The incidence has

---

[1] **defective**: not working properly
[2] **diabetes**: a disease in which the body can't control the level of sugar in the blood
[3] **paediatric obesity**: obesity in children

doubled in the past decade, and worse is to come. A recent report predicted that by 2005, a quarter of British women and almost one-fifth of men will be obese. In much of Europe, 15–20 per cent of the middle-aged population is classifiable as obese. The picture is better for Scandinavia and the Netherlands, where the figure is around 10 per cent, but worse for Eastern Europe, where in some areas it reaches 50 per cent among women. This frequency means that countries such as the UK, France and Germany each have between 5 and 10 million inhabitants who are obese.

The possible consequences of adult obesity include diabetes, high blood pressure, high blood cholesterol, coronary heart disease, sleep apnoea (a life-threatening problem in which breathing stops), gall bladder disease, chronic heartburn, arthritis, certain cancers and depression. Socially, fat people can be as successful as anyone else – think of Santa, for example – but their shape can undermine their self-esteem, particularly in Western societies where thin is fashionable.

Doctors have declared war on obesity. Nowhere is the battle of the bulge more obvious than in America, where obesity leads to an estimated 300,000 deaths each year and costs at least $33 billion per annum in terms of lost working days, health care and other expenditure. Americans spend a further $33 billion a year on weight reduction products and largely ineffective services offered by the slimming industry. This situation has led scientists to ask why we are getting so fat. As a result, new light has been shed on Santa's stomach.

Thousands of years ago, fat meant the difference between life and death: being able to store large quantities of energy-dense fat in the form of adipose (fatty) tissue enabled our ancestors to survive when food was scarce. In the West today, the abundant availability of food and a **sedentary**[1] lifestyle mean that variations in the way individuals balance energy intake and output make some people more at risk of obesity than others.

When more energy is taken in than is burnt by the body during exercise and while maintaining its so-called metabolism (the energy required just to keep it ticking over), the excess is stored as fat. If this continues, obesity will be the eventual result. Studying how we crave, store and use food energy is the key to finding an effective treatment for obesity and perhaps explaining Santa's paunch. Whether you look forward to your Christmas lunch, dread its effect on the waistline, or both, depends on a complicated web of chemical events, from **satiety mechanisms**[2] at work within the brain to the molecular machinery that lays down deposits of fat in cells.

Hunger pangs, whether experienced by Santa or anyone else, are commonly thought to depend on a range of signals, from the sight of the roast turkey and that wonderful aroma, to the first taste of the meat. The conventional belief is that appetite depends on how the body interprets information from the gut and from

[1] **sedentary**: inactive
[2] **satiety mechanisms**: the ways your brain knows when you have eaten enough

hormones in the blood, causing eating habits to be adapted to energy demands. However, since the turn of the century, when it was found that damage to a structure in the brain called the hypothalamus results in obesity, scientists have realised that the urge to eat is caused by something going on in our *heads*. Santa, like the rest of us, is the victim of appetites for food that have been determined by the brain and have evolved in response to the type of diet available during the Stone Age.

Evolution has spent more time **optimising*** our appetite for the food available on the prehistoric African savannah than for today's fast-food culture. As a consequence, appetites evolved to supply the needs of the body in a tough environment where fat and salt were relatively scarce and famine never far away. We have inherited a Stone Age appetite for certain nutrients and, as a consequence, it is easier for us to overeat fats, such as ice-cream, than carbohydrates, such as potatoes, and much easier to overdo carbohydrates than protein. Whereas the protein requirement of primitive humans ranged from 14 to 20 per cent of daily intake, fat appetite was left largely unregulated because immediate energy benefits far outweighed long-term hazards, such as heart disease, which have now become significant as greater numbers of people reach old age ...

Scientists have also discovered that certain genetic defects are linked to obesity, and for this reason, some of

---

***optimising**: maximising

us are more likely to indulge in a Christmas blow-out than others. In people who carry these genes, cravings for fatty food can go on long after the body's capacity to use their calories has been exhausted. Every molecular clue presents a new target for drug designers seeking the **grail*** of the anti-fat pill – and another hint why Santa is so plump.

***grail**: A reference to the Holy Grail, a cup which is said to have held the blood of Jesus Christ. People have searched for the Grail for hundreds of years but it has never been found.

The drowned world

Tim Radford

Global warming is a familiar phrase today but what does it actually mean and how does it affect us? Tim Radford, the science editor of the Guardian, *begins his article with a spoof shipping forecast for June 21 2020 to show how drastic the changes could be and then explores how all aspects of our lives will be affected. As you read:*

- *think about the techniques the author uses to convince the reader of the seriousness of global warming. How effective do you think his methods are?*

Saturday September 11, 2004

The drowned world

Icecaps will be melting, sea levels will be rising ... If you don't like today's weather, says Tim Radford, then wait for the horrors we could face by 2020

"Good morning. Here is the shipping forecast for midday, June 21 2020. Seas will be calm, and visibility will range from good to excellent for the next 24 hours. The sea lanes from Bergen to Tokyo via the north-east passage will largely be free of ice, but occasional small floes may drift near the Siberian coast. The north-west passage from Europe to

15

Fairbanks, Alaska, and Vancouver will also be clear, although iceberg hazards cannot be ruled out between Greenland and Ellesmere Island. The Bering Strait was, for the fourth time in the past decade, free of ice for the entire winter and will remain open for the rest of the summer."

That's just the Arctic. By the summer of 2020, global warming will have had such devastating effect on the northern icecap that European ships may routinely cross the northernmost parts of the world to take the short routes to Asia and the Pacific. The Arctic Ocean, once frozen solid all winter and choked with hazardous **floes**[1] for most of the summer, could be one of the friendlier seas. The **perilous**[2] shortcuts that defied the heroic attempts of the Englishman Martin Frobisher and the Dutchman Willem Barents more than 400 years ago may soon become not just plain sailing, but the standard summer sea route from Europe to the Pacific.

Cruise tourists and shipping magnates might wish to thank global warming. But the chances are they will not. That is because one of the Arctic's great spectacles, the polar bear, will have taken a dive: they need the sea ice to survive. For them, the ice is the way to a diet of seals, walruses and small whales. When the floes go, the polar bear will be on the road to extinction.

The polar bear's base of operations has been shrinking relentlessly as the planet warms. Over the past 40 years, the sheath of ice that covered the Arctic Ocean has

---

[1] **floes**: flat icebergs
[2] **perilous**: dangerous

thinned by 40%. The area covered by ice has also shrunk by more than 25%. Although much climate science is necessarily based on indirect evidence, the state of the Arctic Ocean has been monitored directly by people whose lives depend on the accuracy of their measurements. US, Russian and British nuclear submarines began charting the thickness of Arctic ice at the height of the cold war, and satellite cameras have been recording seasonal changes in ice cover for more than three decades. The conclusions are beyond **dispute*** and the process is unstoppable. By 2020, according to the US Office of Naval Research, the northeast and north-west passages should be navigable. By 2050, according to the UK Hadley Centre for Climate Prediction, the Arctic Ocean could be free of ice in summer.

That will happen because although the planet as a whole is warming perceptibly, the Arctic is warming eight times faster – largely because of a phenomenon called the albedo effect.

Put simply, white reflects light, but dark absorbs it. So the sunlight crashing on to the Arctic and Antarctic ice sheets, the Alpine and tropical glaciers, and the snows of the great mountain chains bounces back into space. In effect, ice is its own insulator: glaciers tend to keep themselves glacial even in the summer.

But once ice starts to melt, dark ocean or rock is exposed. That absorbs the heat, and begins to accelerate the melting process. As long as the average temperatures stay low, there is a natural brake: in high summer, snow evaporates but falls again in winter, to replace the melting

***dispute**: argument

ice and to keep conditions more or less stable. The problem is that things have begun to change. Glaciers in Alaska and the mountains of tropical Africa are in retreat, and climate scientists have predicted that by 2020 the snows of Kilimanjaro and Mount Kenya will have vanished.

In Europe, Alpine economies built on skiing and other mountain sports will have begun to fail. In south Asia, for at least part of the year, snow melt is the only source of water for millions of farmers.

Adventure tourists will lose their holidays. Others stand to lose rather more. On the Indian subcontinent, half a billion people depend on the Indus and Ganges rivers, whose sources lie among melting snows of the Hindu Kush, the Karakoram and the western Himalaya. But these great snowfields, too, are disappearing.

All this is on the basis of an annual global average temperature rise of 0.1C a decade up to now. But it wouldn't take much to make things change faster, and those changes would be irreversible. If global average temperatures rise by more than 2.7C, according to calculations published in *Nature* in April, then the great sheet of ice that covers Greenland will start to melt faster than it can be replaced. The Geological Survey of Greenland and Denmark warned this summer that the ice sheet, which covers 772,000 square miles and is up to two miles thick, is melting 10 times quicker than previously thought. The sheet is thinning at 10 metres per year, not one metre. It could take 1,000 years for the sheet to completely disappear, but as it does so, sea levels will begin to rise by about 7mm a year. Once all the ice has gone, the world's oceans will have risen by around seven metres.

This will happen, because global temperatures seem

likely to rise by far more than 2.7C. Ten years ago, the UN's Intercontinental Panel on Climate Change (IPCC) set up to study global warming proposed a maximum temperature rise of about 3C by 2100. Three years ago, IPCC revised that prediction. The maximum temperature rise during the present century is set at almost 6C. And the predicted maximum temperature rise for Greenland is put at up to 8C.

By 2020, then, the Arctic will have begun to change for ever. The adventure tales of the past will be distant history: stories of explorers fighting their way by sled across the perilous frozen seas will be science fiction to young readers and nostalgic yearnings for a lost world to their parents.

"Here is the long-term weather forecast for the tropical and temperate zones at midday, June 21 2020. After a series of increasingly wet winters, northern Europe could once again be at risk of a lethal heat wave. Forest fires are raging in the Iberian Peninsula, southern France and the Balkans. Water rationing has once again been imposed in California. Relief agencies have warned that late rains raise the spectre of widespread hunger in the Sahel and southern Africa. Bangladesh, however, is once more preparing for catastrophic floods."

It's a matter of simple physics: a warmer world means a rising sea level. Warm water is less dense than cold, so some of the sea level rise will happen just because the water already in the oceans has begun to expand. But sea levels have begun to rise still further with the melting of continental ice and the retreat of the glaciers. The effects of the rise will only slowly become apparent – even the most pessimistic predictions suggest that by 2100 the sea level will only be a metre higher – but even at that slow rate many millions of people will be imperilled. Sea level rise is a threat to anybody who lives at or a fraction above sea level, and especially to citizens of those countries classed as developing. That, of course, means poor.

For such people, the future looks very bleak. There are 54 members of the Commonwealth. Only six of these are classed as developed nations. Around 93% of the Commonwealth lives in the other 48. Some of these countries may have no future at all. "If the scientific forecasts prove correct, then by the end of the century membership of the Commonwealth will have declined because two or three nations will have disappeared," warned Clive Hamilton, director of the Australian Institute, in September 2003. Two Commonwealth states – the Maldives and Tuvalu – are at risk of complete submersion by 2080. Two other groups of islands – Kiribati and the Bahamas – will be in a bad way, because almost all their territories lie below the four-metre mark.

Island dwellers, of course, will not be the only ones at risk. Hundreds of millions of people in densely populated countries with low-lying coastal plains or vast estuaries will come under threat from rising sea levels. According to Sir John Houghton, a former director of the UK Met Office and author of *Global Warming: The Complete Briefing*, a sea level rise of half a metre could sweep away or make uninhabitable about 10% of the habitable land of Bangladesh. That land is currently home to at least six million people. Sea levels will not need to rise by half a metre worldwide to make this happen: the delta region of Bangladesh is subsiding, partly because groundwater is being abstracted for agriculture to feed the nation's 140 million citizens.

By 2050, waters could have risen by a metre,

claiming 20% of Bangladesh and displacing 15 million people. By 2100, the ocean may have encroached up the rivers almost as far as Dhaka, one of the world's fastest growing cities, and across the Indian border to the edge of Calcutta.

A glance around the world shows the same pattern being repeated again and again. In Egypt, a metre rise in the Mediterranean will mean the fertile lands of the Nile delta will disappear beneath the sea, claiming 12% of the country's **arable*** land and displacing seven million people. A sea level rise of half a metre would also cause havoc in the Netherlands and in the Mississippi delta. But the difference between those two regions and those in the developing world is that the Dutch and the Americans already spend money on sea defences and can afford more. In China, a half-metre rise in the sea level could flood the plains of the eastern coast, covering an area of land the size of the Netherlands, leaving 30 million homeless.

And if the sea doesn't get you, the storms will. Hurricanes and cyclones are freak events whose existence is controlled by sea temperatures. If the surface temperature of the ocean is below 26.5C, typhoons, tropical cyclones and hurricanes hardly happen. But with each rise in temperature beyond that point they become more frequent and more ferocious. Savage storms, and the sea surges they bring, will pose huge threats to small island states and could scour low-lying land completely clear.

Twenty years ago, climate scientists warned that in a greenhouse world, the kind of fierce storms that had been once-a-century occurrences would come around every decade. The fatal combination of very high tide

---

***arable**: crop farming

and tropical cyclone has hit Bangladesh and the Bengal coast of India many times. In 1991, one such storm surge claimed an estimated 139,000 lives. In 1970, another killed 300,000 people. UN researchers warned in June that an estimated one billion people live in the path of the kind of flood that used to occur every 100 years: by 2050, the number of potential victims could reach two billion.

If two billion people are at risk of dramatic **inundation**[1] in 2020, around 2.3 billion others living in the world's water-poor nations could face an even more wretched future. They will see increasingly **parched**[2] landscapes, empty wells, polluted lakes and rivers that run dry. UN experts calculated that in 2000, people in 30 nations faced water shortages. By 2020, they predict, that number will have risen to 50 nations.

As temperatures rise, more water will evaporate, but rainfall will remain unpredictable. Countries in the monsoon belt will face more severe droughts in the dry season but could also have to deal with more catastrophic flooding. Other regions – the southern Mediterranean, north Africa, southern Africa and the Sahel – could become even more dry. The great plains of North America, the breadbasket for the planet, could turn again into a dustbowl, delivering less and less grain to a world that acquires an extra 240,000 mouths to feed every single day.

The pattern of falling crop yields will be seen all over the planet. They are expected to decline by at least 10% in most African Commonwealth countries, and by even more in Mozambique, Tanzania, Botswana and Namibia. There could also be dramatic falls in food production in

---

[1] **inundation**: flooding
[2] **parched**: extremely dry

India, Pakistan and Bangladesh, although harvests could increase by 10% in Brunei, Malaysia, Singapore and Papua New Guinea. Canada and New Zealand could also see dramatic increases in crop yields but Australia, already largely arid, will be one of the economic losers.

And forget the remarks about the one good side-effect of global warming being decent summers. In 2003, more than 20,000 people died in northern Europe because of a heat wave that saw Germany roasting in its hottest temperatures for 450 years. Climate scientists believe that if atmospheric warming continues unchecked, such heat waves can be expected every 20 years or so – so expect summer 2020 to be every bit as oppressive as last year.

"The summer of 2003 was a summer of the future," said Gerhard Berz, head of natural risks research at Munich Re, one of the insurance giants that has to calculate hazard and pick up the bill for floods, heat waves, ice storms, hurricanes, forest fires and droughts.

Global warming is expected to bring good news for some. But right now it looks like it will be delivering bad news to most people by 2020. The IPCC, the international group of climate scientists that has delivered increasingly urgent warnings since it was established in 1988, is that rare thing: a group of scientists who would love to be proved wrong. Their predictions have been made in the hope that governments will take action, and in doing so direct the planet towards a less fearful future. There is evidence that governments have been listening.

Action, however, has been slow. Acting now would be too late to avert the challenges of 2020. We are starting to see the effects of carbon emissions of a few decades ago: your fuel-efficient small car is an investment in the future, because we're currently paying for that great gas guzzler your family was driving in the 70s. Every cook who knows a bit about science understands a concept called thermal inertia: the gas is on full, but the kettle takes a few minutes to boil, and though the gas is off, it takes a while to cool down. We're still waiting for the earth to start simmering, but by 2020 the bubbles will be appearing, whatever we do today.

The Edge of the Sea

Rachel Carson

In this extract Rachel Carson, a marine zoologist and environmentalist, describes the sea shore of the Florida coast and reflects on how the varied life there has changed over millions of years. People often think of literature and science as very different, but many writers combine an interest in both. Although her writing deals with serious scientific subjects it is very personal and poetic in style. As you read:

- *think about the words she uses to describe the landscape. How do they reveal her feelings about nature? How do they make you feel?*

The edge of the sea is a strange and beautiful place. All through the long history of earth it has been an area of unrest where waves have broken heavily against the land, where the tides have pressed forward over the continents, receded, and then returned. For no two successive days is the shore line precisely the same. Not only do the tides advance and retreat in their eternal rhythms, but the level of the sea itself is never at rest. It rises or falls as the glaciers melt or grow, as the floor of the deep ocean basins shifts … or as the earth's crust … warps up or down in adjustment to strain and tension. Today a little more land may belong to the sea, tomorrow a little less. Always the edge of the sea remains an **elusive**[1] and indefinable boundary.

The shore has a dual nature, changing with the swing of the tides, belonging now to the land, now to the sea. On the **ebb tide**[2] it knows the harsh extremes of the land world, being exposed to heat and cold, to wind, to rain and drying sun. On the **flood tide**[3] it is a water world, returning briefly to the relative stability of the open sea.

Only the most hardy and adaptable can survive in a region so [changeable], yet the area between the tide lines is crowded with plants and animals. In this difficult world of the shore, life displays its enormous toughness and vitality by occupying almost every conceivable niche. Visibly, it carpets the intertidal rocks; or half hidden, it descends into **fissures and crevices**[4], or hides under boulders, or lurks in the wet gloom of sea caves. Invisibly, where the casual observer would say there is no life, it lies deep in the sand, in burrows and tubes and passageways. It tunnels into solid rock and bores into peat and clay...

In my thoughts of the shore, one place stands apart for its revelation of exquisite beauty. It is a pool hidden within a cave that one can visit only rarely and briefly when the lowest of the year's low tides fall below it, and perhaps from that very fact it acquires some of its special beauty. Choosing such a tide, I hoped for a glimpse of the pool...

---

[1] **elusive**: difficult to find

[2] **ebb tide**: outward tide

[3] **flood tide**: inward tide

[4] **fissures and crevices**: gaps and cracks in the rock

I stood above the tide near the entrance to the pool… From the base of the steep wall of rock on which I stood, a moss-covered ledge jutted seaward into deep water. In the surge at the rim of the ledge the oarweeds swayed, smooth and gleaming as leather. The projecting ledge was the path to the small hidden cave and its pool. Occasionally a swell, stronger than the rest, rolled smoothly over the rim and broke in foam against the cliff. But the intervals between such swells were long enough to admit me to the ledge and long enough for a glimpse of that fairy pool, so seldom and so briefly exposed…

The floor of the cave was only a few inches below the roof, and a mirror had been created in which all that grew on the ceiling was reflected in the still water below.

Under water that was clear as glass the pool was carpeted with green sponge. Gray patches of sea squirts glistened on the ceiling and colonies of soft coral were a pale apricot colour. In the moment when I looked into the cave a little elfin starfish hung down, suspended by the merest thread, perhaps by only a single tube foot. It reached down to touch its own reflection, so perfectly delineated that there might have been, not one starfish, but two. The beauty of the reflected images and of the **limpid**[1] pool itself was the **poignant**[2] beauty of things that are **ephemeral**[3], existing only until the sea should return to fill the little cave…

---

[1] **limpid**: clear
[2] **poignant**: moving (emotionally)
[3] **ephemeral**: short lived

The sense of creation comes with memories of a southern coast, where the sea and the mangroves, working together, are building a wilderness of thousands of small islands off the south-western coast of Florida, separated from each other by a tortuous pattern of bays, lagoons, and narrow waterways. I remember a winter day when the sky was blue and drenched with sunlight; though there was no wind one was conscious of flowing air like cold clear crystal. I had landed on the surf-washed tip of one of those islands, and then worked my way around to the sheltered bay side. There I found the tide far out, exposing the broad mud flat of a cove bordered by the mangroves with their twisted branches, their glossy leaves, and their long prop roots reaching down, grasping and holding the mud, building the land out a little more, then again a little more…

The drift of time [was] quietly summarized in the existence of hundreds of small snails – the mangrove periwinkles – browsing on the branches and roots of the trees. Once their ancestors had been sea dwellers, bound to the salt waters by every tie of their life processes. Little by little over the thousands and millions of years the ties had been broken, the snails had adjusted themselves to life out of water, and now today they were living many feet above the tide to which they only occasionally returned. And perhaps, who could say how many ages [in the future], there would be in their descendants not even this gesture of remembrance for the sea…

There is a common thread that links these scenes and memories – the spectacle of life in all its varied manifestations as it has appeared, evolved, and sometimes died out… It sends us back to the edge of the sea, where the drama of life played its first scene on earth and … where the forces of evolution are at work today, as they have been since the appearance of what we know as life.

The sea before time

Dava Sobel

Today we take it for granted that we can work out exactly where we are at any point on the globe. In the past, particularly at sea, there was a large amount of guesswork involved. While it was possible to work out a ship's latitude (the position on the globe north or south of the equator), nobody knew how to work out longitude (the position on the globe east of west of a meridian, a vertical line running from the North to South Pole). Because of this, many ships were wrecked and many lives lost. In this extract, Dava Sobel tells the dramatic story of the shipwreck in 1707 which led the British government to offer a prize of £20,000 (the equivalent of several million pounds today) to anyone who could solve the problem of how to measure longitude precisely. As you read:

- *think about how the writer captures the reader's interest through the use of personal stories to make the account vivid.*

'Dirty weather', Admiral Sir Clowdisley Shovell called the fog that had dogged him twelve days at sea. Returning home victorious from Gibraltar after **skirmishes*** with the French Mediterranean forces, Sir Clowdisley could not beat the heavy autumn overcast. Fearing the ships might founder on coastal rocks, the admiral summoned all his

***skirmishes**: short battles

navigators to put their heads together.

The **consensus**[1] opinion placed the English fleet safely west of Île d'Ouessant, an island outpost of the Brittany peninsula. But as the sailors continued north, they discovered to their horror that they had miscalculated their longitude near the Scilly Isles. These tiny islands, about twenty miles from the southwest tip of England, point to Land's End like a path of stepping-stones. And on that foggy night of October 22, 1707, the Scillies became unmarked tombstones for two thousand of Sir Clowdisley's troops.

The flagship, the *Association*, struck first. She sank within minutes, drowning all **hands**[2]. Before the rest of the vessels could react to the obvious danger, two more ships, the *Eagle* and the *Romney*, pricked themselves on the rocks and went down like stones. In all, four of the five warships were lost.

Only two men washed ashore alive. One of them was Sir Clowdisley himself, who may have watched the fifty-seven years of his life flash before his eyes as the waves carried him home. Certainly he had time to reflect on the events of the previous twenty-four hours, when he made what must have been the worst mistake in judgment of his naval career. He had been approached by a sailor, a member of the *Association*'s crew, who claimed to have kept his own reckoning of the fleet's location during the

---

[1] **consensus**: majority
[2] **hands**: sailors

whole cloudy passage. Such **subversive**[1] navigation by an inferior was forbidden in the Royal Navy, as the unnamed seaman well knew. However, the danger appeared so enormous, by his calculations, that he risked his neck to make his concerns known to the officers. Admiral Shovell had the man hanged for mutiny on the spot.

No one was around to spit 'I told you so!' into Sir Clowdisley's face as he nearly drowned. But as soon as the admiral collapsed on dry sand, a local woman combing the beach **purportedly**[2] found his body and fell in love with the emerald ring on his finger. Between her desire and his **depletion**[3], she handily murdered him for it. Three decades later, on her deathbed, this same woman confessed the crime to her clergyman, producing the ring as proof of her guilt and **contrition**[4].

The demise of Sir Clowdisley's fleet capped a long saga of seafaring in the days before sailors could find their longitude. Page after page from this miserable history relates typical horror stories of death by scurvy and thirst, of ghosts in the rigging, and of landfalls in the form of shipwrecks, with hulls dashed on rocks and heaps of drowned corpses fouling the beaches. In literally hundreds of instances, a vessel's ignorance of her longitude led swiftly to her destruction.

---

[1] **subversive**: rebellious

[2] **purportedly**: apparently

[3] **depletion**: weakness

[4] **contrition**: regret

Launched on a mix of bravery and greed, the sea captains of the fifteenth, sixteenth, and seventeenth centuries relied on 'dead reckoning' to calculate their distance east or west of home port. The captain would throw a log overboard and observe how quickly the ship receded from this temporary guidepost. He noted the crude speedometer reading in his ship's logbook, along with the direction of travel, which he took from the stars or a compass, and the length of time on a particular course, counted with a sandglass or a pocket watch. Factoring in the effects of ocean currents, **fickle**[1] winds, and errors in judgment, he then **determined**[2] his longitude. He routinely missed his mark, of course – searching in vain for the island where he had hoped to find fresh water, or even the continent that was his destination. Too often, the technique of dead reckoning marked him for a dead man.

Long voyages lasted longer for lack of longitude, and the extra time at sea condemned sailors to the dread disease of scurvy. The oceangoing diet of the day, completely lacking fresh fruits and vegetables, deprived them of vitamin C, and their bodies' connective tissue deteriorated as a result. Their blood vessels leaked, making the men look bruised all over, even in the absence of any injury. When they were injured, their wounds failed to heal. Their legs swelled. They suffered the pain of

---

[1] **fickle**: changeable

[2] **determined**: worked out

spontaneous bleeding into their muscles and joints. Their gums bled, too, as their teeth loosened. They gasped for breath, struggled against debilitating weakness, and when the blood vessels around their brains ruptured, they died.

Beyond this potential for human suffering, the global ignorance of longitude caused economic havoc on the grandest scale. It confined oceangoing vessels to a few narrow shipping lanes that promised safe passage. Forced to navigate by latitude alone, whaling ships, merchant ships, warships, and pirate ships all clustered along well-trafficked routes, where they fell prey to one another. In 1592, for example, a squadron of six English **men-of-war**[1] waited off the Azores, lying in ambush for Spanish traders heading back from the Caribbean. The *Madre de Deus*, an enormous Portuguese galleon returning from India, sailed into their web. Despite her thirty-two brass guns, the *Madre de Deus* lost the brief battle, and Portugal lost a princely cargo. Under the ship's hatches lay chests of gold and silver coins, pearls, diamonds, amber, musk, tapestries, calico, and ebony. The spices had to be counted by the ton – more than four hundred tons of pepper, forty-five of cloves, thirty-five of cinnamon, and three each of mace and nutmeg. The *Madre de Deus* proved herself a prize worth half a million pounds sterling – or approximately half the net value of the entire English **Exchequer**[2] at that date.

---

[1] **men-of-war**: battleships

[2] **Exchequer**: economy

By the end of the seventeenth century, nearly three hundred ships a year sailed between the British Isles and the West Indies to ply the Jamaica trade. Since the sacrifice of a single one of these cargo vessels caused terrible losses, merchants yearned to avoid the inevitable. They wished to discover secret routes – and that meant discovering a means to determine longitude.

The disastrous wreck on the Scillies, so close to the shipping centres of England, catapulted the longitude question into the forefront of national affairs. The sudden loss of so many lives, so many ships, and so much honour all at once, on top of centuries of previous hardships, underscored the **folly*** of ocean navigation without a means for finding longitude. The souls of Sir Clowdisley's lost sailors – another two thousand martyrs to the cause – brought about the famed Longitude Act of 1714, in which Parliament promised a prize of £20,000 for a solution to the longitude problem.

In 1736, an unknown clockmaker named John Harrison carried a promising possibility on a trial voyage to Lisbon aboard H.M.S. *Centurion*. The ship's officers saw firsthand how Harrison's clock could improve their reckoning. Indeed, they thanked Harrison when his newfangled contraption showed them to be about sixty miles off course on the way home to London.

By September 1740, however, when the *Centurion* set sail for the South Pacific under the command of Commodore

---

***folly**: stupidity

George Anson, the longitude clock stood on **terra firma**[1] in Harrison's house at Red Lion Square. There the inventor, having already completed an improved second version of it, was hard at work on a third with further refinements. But such devices were not yet generally accepted, and would not become generally available for another fifty years. So Anson's squadron took the Atlantic the old-fashioned way, on the strength of latitude readings, dead reckoning, and good seamanship. The fleet reached **Patagonia**[2] intact, after an unusually long crossing, but then a grand tragedy unfolded, founded on the loss of their longitude at sea.

On March 7, 1741, with the holds already stinking of scurvy, Anson sailed the *Centurion* through the Straits Le Maire, from the Atlantic into the Pacific Ocean. As he rounded the tip of Cape Horn, a storm blew up from the west. It shredded the sails and pitched the ship so violently that men who lost their holds were dashed to death. The storm **abated**[3] from time to time only to regather its strength, and punished the *Centurion* for fifty-eight days without mercy. The winds carried rain, sleet, and snow. And scurvy all the while whittled away at the crew, killing six to ten men every day.

Anson held west against this onslaught, more or less along the parallel at sixty degrees south latitude, until he

---

[1] **terra firma**: solid ground

[2] **Patagonia**: an area in Argentina and Chile

[3] **abated**: calmed down

figured he had gone a full two hundred miles westward, beyond Tierra del Fuego. The other five ships of his squadron had been separated from the *Centurion* in the storm, and some of them were lost forever.

On the first moonlit night he had seen in two months, Anson at last anticipated calm waters, and steered north for the earthly paradise called Juan Fernández Island. There he knew he would find fresh water for his men, to soothe the dying and sustain the living. Until then, they would have to survive on hope alone, for several days of sailing on the vast Pacific still separated them from the island oasis. But as the haze cleared, Anson sighted *land* right away, dead ahead. It was Cape Noir, at the western edge of Tierra del Fuego.

How could this have happened? Had they been sailing in reverse?

The fierce currents had thwarted Anson. All the time he thought he was gaining westward, he had been virtually treading water. So he had no choice but to head west *again*, then north toward salvation. He knew that if he failed, and if the sailors continued dying at the same rate, there wouldn't be enough hands left to man the rigging.

According to the ship's log, on May 24, 1741, Anson at last delivered the *Centurion* to the latitude of Juan Fernández Island, at thirty-five degrees south. All that remained to do was to run down the parallel to make harbour. But which way should he go? Did the island lie to the east or to the west of the *Centurion*'s present position?

That was anybody's guess.

Anson guessed west, and so headed in that direction. Four more desperate days at sea, however, stripped him of the courage of his conviction, and he turned the ship around.

Forty-eight hours after the *Centurion* began beating east along the thirty-fifth parallel, land was sighted! But it showed itself to be the **impermeable***, Spanish-ruled, mountain-walled coast of Chile. This jolt required a one-hundred-eighty-degree change in direction, and in Anson's thinking. He was forced to confess that he had probably been within hours of Juan Fernández Island when he abandoned west for east. Once again, the ship had to retrace her course.

On June 9, 1741, the *Centurion* dropped anchor at last at Juan Fernández. The two weeks of zigzag searching for the island had cost Anson an additional eighty lives. Although he was an able navigator who could keep his ship at her proper depth and protect his crew from mass drowning, his delays had given scurvy the upper hand. Anson helped carry the hammocks of sick sailors ashore, then watched helplessly as the scourge picked off his men one by one … by one by one, until more than half of the original five hundred were dead and gone.

***impermeable**: inaccessible

Family and childhood

We have all experienced childhood so we all have personal histories and memories to bring to these texts. The writers of these extracts have to meet the challenge of how to make their own personal experiences relevant, engaging and thought-provoking for all readers; even those readers who do not share the same life histories. To do this, some of the writers in this collection describe the characters that feature in their writing in close detail, clearly recreating the scenes and personalities for us. Others use humour to reveal aspects of an event or a person to us and others write factually about something we all recognise and can identify with. As you read these extracts, think about what these writers have done to engage your interest. Question why they have selected the particular details they include and what this reveals to us about their view of family life or of childhood. Look closely at the language they have chosen. How do their characters reveal themselves through the things they say? How is language used to paint a picture of a scene or an event and make it memorable for the reader?

Oulton Park

Blake Morrison

Writing well about a real person is difficult and different from writing about someone you have imagined – especially if it is someone you know well. In his book, And When Did You Last See Your Father?, *the writer Blake Morrison tells the story of his father's life and death from cancer with honesty and affection. In this extract Morrison recalls an episode from his childhood which conveys many of his father's qualities, both endearing and exasperating. As you read:*
- *think about the techniques Morrison uses to build a vivid and humorous picture of his father.*

A hot September Saturday in 1959, and we are stationary in Cheshire. Ahead of us, a queue of cars stretches out of sight around the corner. We haven't moved for ten minutes. Everyone has turned his engine off, and now my father does so too. In the sudden silence we can hear the distant whinge of what must be the first race of the afternoon, a ten-lap event for saloon cars. It is quarter past one. In an hour the drivers will be warming up for the main event, the Gold Cup – Graham Hill, Jack Brabham, Roy Salvadori, Stirling Moss and Joakim Bonnier. My father has always loved fast cars, and motor-racing has a strong British following just now, which is why we are stuck here in this country lane with hundreds of other cars.

My father does not like waiting in queues. He is used to patients waiting in queues to see him, but he is not used to waiting in queues himself. A queue, to him, means a man being denied the right to be where he wants to be at a time of his own choosing, which is at the front, now. Ten minutes have passed. What is happening up ahead? What fathead has caused this snarl-up? Why are no cars coming the other way? Has there been an accident? Why are there no police to sort it out? Every two minutes or so my father gets out of the car, crosses to the opposite verge and tries to see if there is movement up ahead. There isn't. He gets back in and steams some more. The roof of our Alvis is down, the sun beating on to the leather upholstery, the chrome, the picnic basket. The hood is folded and pleated into the mysterious crevice between the boot and the narrow back seat where my sister and I are scrunched together as usual. The roof is nearly always down, whatever the weather: my father loves fresh air, and every car he has owned has been a convertible, so that he can have fresh air. But the air today is not fresh. There is a **pall*** of high-rev exhaust, dust, petrol, boiling-over engines.

In the cars ahead and behind, people are laughing, eating sandwiches, drinking from beer bottles, enjoying the weather, settling into the familiar indignity of waiting-to-get-to-the-front. But my father is not like them. There are only two things on his mind: the invisible head of the

---

***pall**: cloud-like covering

queue and, not unrelated, the other half of the country lane, tantalizingly empty.

'Just relax, Arthur,' my mother says. 'You're in and out of the car like a blue-tailed fly.'

But being told to relax only **incenses*** him. 'What can it be?' he demands. 'Maybe there's been an accident. Maybe they're waiting for an ambulance.' We all know where this last speculation is leading, even before he says it. 'Maybe they need a doctor.'

'No, Arthur,' says my mother, as he opens the door again and stands on the wheel-arch to crane ahead.

'It must be an accident,' he announces. 'I think I should drive up and see.'

'No, Arthur. It's just the number waiting to get in. And surely there must be doctors on the circuit.'

It is one-thirty and silent now. The saloon race has finished. It is still over an hour until the Gold Cup itself, but there's another race first, and the cars in the paddock to see, and besides…

'Well, I'm not going to bloody well wait here any longer,' he says. 'We'll never get in. We might as well turn round and give up.' He sits there for another twenty seconds, then leans forward, opens the glove compartment and pulls out a stethoscope, which he hooks over the mirror on the windscreen. It hangs there like a skeleton, the membrane at the top, the metal and rubber leads dangling bow-legged, the two ivory earpieces

---

***incenses**: infuriates

clopping bonily against each other. He starts the engine, releases the handbrake, reverses two feet, then pulls out into the opposite side of the road.

'No,' says my mother again, half-heartedly. It could be that he is about to do a three-point turn and go back. No it couldn't...

My father does not drive particularly quickly past the marooned cars ahead. No more than twenty miles an hour. Even so, it *feels* fast, and arrogant, and all the occupants turn and stare as they see us coming. Some appear to be angry. Some are shouting. 'Point to the stethoscope, pet,' he tells my mother, but she has slid down sideways in her passenger seat, out of sight, her bottom resting on the floor, from where she berates him.

'God Almighty, Arthur, why do you have to do this? Why can't you wait like everyone else? What if we meet something coming the other way?' Now my sister and I do the same, hide ourselves below the seat. Our father is on his own. He is not with us, this bullying, shaming, undemocratic cheat. Or rather, we are not with him.

My face pressed to the sweet-smelling upholstery, I imagine what is happening ahead. I can't tell how far we have gone, how many blind corners we have taken. If we meet something, on this narrow country lane, we will have to reverse past all the cars we have just overtaken. That's if we can stop in time. I wait for the squeal of brakes, the clash of metal.

After an eternity of – what? – two minutes, my mother sticks her head up and says, 'Now you've had it,' and my father replies, 'No, there's another gate beyond,' and my sister and I raise ourselves to look. We are up level with the cars at the head of the queue, which are waiting to turn left into the brown ticket holders' entrance, the plebs' entrance. A steward steps out of the gateway towards us, but my father, pretending not to see him, doesn't stop. He drives ahead, on to a clear piece of road where, two hundred yards away, half a dozen cars from the opposite direction are waiting to turn into another gateway. Unlike those we have left behind, these cars appear to be moving. Magnanimous, my father waits until the last of them has turned in, then drives through the stone gateposts and over the bumpy grass to where an armbanded steward in a tweed jacket is waiting by the roped entrance.

'Good afternoon, sir. Red ticket holder?' The question does not come as a shock: we have seen the signs, numerous and clamorous, saying RED TICKET HOLDERS' ENTRANCE. But my father is undeterred.

'These, you mean,' he says, and hands over his brown tickets.

'No, sir, I'm afraid these are brown tickets.'

'But there must be some mistake. I applied for red tickets. To be honest, I didn't even look.'

'I'm sorry, sir, but these are brown tickets, and brown's the next entrance, two hundred yards along. If you just swing round here, and ...'

'I'm happy to pay the difference.'

'No, you see the rules say... .'

'I know where the brown entrance is, I've just spent the

44

last hour queuing for it by mistake. I drove up here because I thought I was red. I can't go back there now. The queue stretches for miles. And these children, you know, who'd been looking forward....'

By now, half a dozen cars have gathered behind us. One of them parps. The steward is wavering.

'You say you applied for red.'

'Not only applied for, paid for. I'm a doctor, you see' – he points at the stethoscope – 'and I like being near the grand-stand'.

This double **non-sequitur**[1] seems to clinch it.

'All right, sir, but next time please check the tickets. Ahead and to your right.'

This is the way it was with my father. Minor **duplicities**[2]. Little fiddles. Money-saving, time-saving, privilege-attaining fragments of opportunism. The queue-jump, the backhander, the deal under the table. Parking where you shouldn't, drinking after hours, accepting the poached pheasant and the goods off the back of a lorry. 'They' were killjoys, after all – 'they' meaning the establishment to which, despite being a middle-class professional, a GP, he didn't belong; our job, as ordinary folk trying to get the most out of life, was to outwit them. Serious lawbreaking would have scared him, though he envied and often praised to us those who had pulled off ingenious crimes, like the Great Train Robbers or, before

---

[1] **non-sequitur**: a statement which is not connected to what was said before
[2] **duplicities**: dishonest acts

them, the men who intercepted a lorry carrying a large number of old bank-notes to the incinerator ('Still in currency, you see, but not new so there was no record of the numbers and they couldn't be traced. Nobody got hurt, either. Brilliant, quite brilliant'). He was not himself up to being criminal in a big way, but he was lost if he couldn't cheat in a small way: so much of his pleasure derived from it. I grew up thinking it absolutely normal, that most Englishmen were like this. I still suspect that's the case.

My childhood was a web of little scams and triumphs. The time we stayed at a hotel situated near the fifth tee of a famous golf-course – Troon, was it? – and discovered that if we started at the fifth hole and finished at the fourth we could avoid the clubhouse and green fees. The private tennis clubs and yacht clubs and drinking clubs we got into (especially on Sundays in dry counties of Wales) by giving someone else's name: by the time the man on the door had failed to find it, my father would have read the names on the list upside-down – 'There, see, Wilson – no Wilson, I said, not Watson'; if all else failed, you could try slipping the chap a one-pound note. With his innocence, confidence and hail-fellow cheeriness, my father could usually talk his way into anything, and usually, when caught, out of anything.

He failed only once. We were on holiday, skiing, in Aviemore, and he treated us to a drink in one of the posher hotels. On his way back from the lavatories, he noticed a sauna room for residents near a small back entrance. For the rest of the week, we sneaked in to enjoy residents' saunas. On the last day, though, we were towelling ourselves dry when an angry manager walked in: 'You're not residents, are you?'

I waited for some artless reply – 'You mean the saunas aren't open to the pubic, like the bars? I thought...' – but for once my father stammered and looked guilty. We ended up paying some **exorbitant**[1] sum *and* being banned from the hotel. I was **indignant**[2]. I discovered he was **fallible**[3]. I felt conned.

Oulton Park, half an hour later. We have met up with our cousins in the brown car park – they of course got here on time – and brought them back to the entrance to the paddock. My father has assumed that, with the red tickets he's wangled, we are entitled to enter the paddock for nothing, along with our guests. He is wrong. Tickets to the paddock cost a guinea. There are ten of us. We're talking serious money.

'We'll buy *one*, anyway,' my father is saying to the man in the ticket-booth, and he comes back with it, a small brown paper card, like a library ticket, with a piece of string attached to a hole at the top so you can thread it through your lapel. 'Let me just investigate,' he says, and disappears through the gate, the steward seeing the lapel-ticket and nodding him through: no stamp on the hand or name-check. In ten minutes or so my father is back. He whispers to my Uncle Ron, hands him the ticket and leads

---

[1] **exorbitant**: unreasonably expensive

[2] **indignant**: angry

[3] **fallible**: able to make mistakes

the rest of us to a wooden-slatted fence in a quiet corner of the car park. Soon Uncle Ron appears on the other side of the fence, in an equally quiet corner of the paddock, and passes the ticket through the slats. Cousin Richard takes the ticket this time and repeats the procedure. One by one we all troop round: Kela, Auntie Mary, Edward, Jane, Gillian, my mother, me. In five minutes, all ten of us are inside.

'Marvellous,' my father says. 'Three pounds eleven shillings and we've got four red tickets and ten of us in the paddock. That'd be costing anyone else twenty guineas. Not bad.'

We stand round Jack Brabham's Cooper, its bonnet opened like a body on an operating table, a mass of tubes and wires and gleamy bits of white and silver. I touch the metal behind the cockpit and think of my green Dinky car, no. 8, which I call Jack Brabham in the races I have on the carpet against the red Ferrari no. 1 (Fangio) and the silver Maserati no. 3 (Salvadori) and the yellow Jaguar no. 4 (Stirling Moss). I like Jack Brabham to win, and somehow he always does, though I swear I push the cars equally. It is quiet at home, pretending. Here at Oulton Park it's not quiet: there's a headachy mix of petrol and sun and engine roar.

Later, Moss overtakes Brabham on lap six, and stays there for the next sixty-nine laps. A car comes off the circuit between Lodge Corner and Deer Leap, just along from where we're standing. There is blood, splintered wood and broken glass. My father disappears – 'just to see if I can help.' He comes back strangely quiet, and whispers to my mother: 'Nothing I could do.'

Toys Were Us

Nicholas Whittaker

How do crazes for new toys start? Is it big business or children's imagination that is in control? In this extract from Toys Were Us: A Twentieth Century History of Toys, *Nicholas Whittaker describes how toy manufacturers market their products in an attempt to create a craze amongst children for a new toy. But are the toys really that new? And do things really change all that much? As you read:*

- *think about how Whittaker structures his ideas. Do you find his argument convincing?*

As a parent, I can't help thinking that children today have less *fun* than we had. Their lives seem dominated by the race to acquire, to compete with a peer group that has no leader except some figure on TV, a figure who could be viewed as being equally manufactured and slickly marketed as the toys. Once the marketing machine cranks up around October, the kids don't stand a chance. Assaulted on all sides by TV ads, catalogues and their friends, they end up with their heads spinning faster than Linda Blair in *The Exorcist*. Choice has always been agonising, but now it is more so.

There's a wonderful irony in *Toy Story*. Its heroes are a bunch of traditional 1950s and 1960s toys who have been neglected in tear-jerking 'Puff the Magic Dragon' fashion.

Mr Potato Head, a cowboy, a springy sausage dog, these are the toys that the new generation had turned its back on. But as heroes of a Hollywood blockbuster they became marketable commodities once again, with millions of kids clamouring for their own copies. Maybe that's what gave the film its appeal to adults – a warm glow brought on by the **meting out of poetic justice**[1]. The double irony is that these lovable characters were all computer-generated, with not a loose thread, dodgy stuffing or peculiar odour about any of them. Antiseptic and digitally perfect, they nevertheless alerted kids to a lovability that they were missing out on.

Steam engines aren't lovable, it seems, unless they have Thomas's grinning face on the smokebox door. If in doubt, stick a smiley face on it. The craze for spotting Eddie Stobart lorries has now filtered down to the shelves of Britain's toyshops. It is a sad reflection on society that the child strapped into his car seat like a trussed-up turkey has no better pastime than to spot this man's lorries, but we can't really blame Mr Stobart for that. However, having his lorries glorified isn't quite enough: Steady Eddie is now a fully fledged cartoon character and his lorry toys now come saddled with Steady Eddie's beaming **fizzog**[2]. This tendency to cuteness in toys may be disturbing, but any parent would prefer it to another growing trend: obsessive collecting.

---

[1] **meting out of poetic justice**: when something happens that seems well deserved, often in an ironic manner
[2] **fizzog**: face

Cuddly and adorable with big goo-goo eyes, Beanie Babies like Pouch the Kangaroo, Spike the Rhinoceros and Claude the Crab wanted to be your special friend. They were the invention of Ty Warner, a fifty-five-year-old media-shy billionaire known as the **Howard Hughes**[1] of the toy industry. As the sole owner of his company, the 250 million Beanie Babies sold in 1998 earned Warner the rather spooky title of 'Richest Toy-maker in the World' – estimated to be worth some seven billion dollars. The company's smart but **forbidding**[2] office block in Chicago has no postal address other than a PO box. The phone number is ex-directory and trespassers are warned off. Staff were obliged to sign a secrecy pledge before joining the company, vowing never to discuss their boss or any aspect of the company's operations. Business associates were allowed to communicate only in writing. Since media sleuths could trace only two photographs of Ty Warner, there were doubts that he even existed.

Animals like Squealer the Pig and Pinchers the Lobster sold for around four pounds in the shops, but rare editions could fetch up to £1,250 on the black market. Collectors and criminals both gambled on the toys becoming prized. A massive second-hand trade grew up, fuelled by the Internet and prices spiralled. Billionaire Bear, created to celebrate one billion dollars' worth of Beanies sold, is now worth more than two thousand dollars itself. A Princess

---

[1] **Howard Hughes**: a famous film producer who became a recluse in later life
[2] **forbidding**: gloomy and uninviting

Bear, in memory of the late Princess of Wales, earned nearly seven million pounds for her memorial fund. When McDonald's gave away mini-Beanie Babies with their Happy Meals their supply – bought to last throughout the six-week promotion – was exhausted in three days. Clever marketeers increased the demand simply by restricting supplies. Beanie Babies were never advertised, nor sold in major toyshop chains such as Toys R Us. Since their debut in 1994, they were available only through small gift shops, and each design was 'retired' quickly, making older ones sought after.

In 1999 Warner stunned the toy industry by announcing that Beanie Babies were for the chop. No explanation was given. Speculation was rife. Why would Warner want to kill off a golden goose that had earned him billions and could yet earn him many times more? Spokesmen refused to elaborate, save to acknowledge that media reports of criminal activity had been a factor.

The final Beanie Baby, a small black bear, was known appropriately as The End.

No sooner had he departed the toyshops than the shelves were stacked with another money-spinner with seemingly limitless potential for profit. Pokémon was almost instantly denounced by US police as America's 'most dangerous hobby' – quite a claim from a country where sub-machine-guns are freely available for recreation. But as commercial hysteria and hard-nosed values filtered down from the adult world into schools and playgrounds, Pokémon cards were blamed for a wave of stabbings, beatings and robbings as kids strove to collect all the sets. If they couldn't get their cards fair and square they might as well take someone else's. 'It's become a war because such huge amounts of money are involved,' said an LA cop. 'Kids are literally fighting each other to get their hands on these cards.'

'This is far worse than the Cabbage Patch Doll craze,' said a policeman in Philadelphia after six children were arrested for attacks on classmates. 'There are Pokémon **card sharps**[1] out there.' In California prosecutors filed charges against a thirteen-year-old boy from Orange County who was accused of stealing a classmate's Pokémon cards – and then running him over with his bicycle.

Bad publicity had dogged Pokémon from the start, even before it was exported to the West. In 1997 hundreds of Japanese children suffered seizures triggered by the flashing of the Pikachu character's lightning bolt on the Pokémon TV cartoons.

Pokémon – short for pocket monsters (and spookily **prescient**[2]) – was the brainchild of Satoshi Tajiri, a Japanese games inventor who combined his childhood loves of monster movies and **entomology**[3]. The game involves 155 creatures, each with its own special powers. The goal is to win as many of the colourful cards from opponents as possible.

---

[1] **card sharps**: people who cheat at cards to win money
[2] **prescient**: predicting the future
[3] **entomology**: the study of insects

While the appeal of Pokémon remained baffling to adults, a Nintendo spokesman gave his own interpretation: 'Pikachu and the other Pokémon characters look very cute, but if anything happens then they are ready to fight. Maybe that is why they appeal to Americans.'

But a simple card game is no longer enough to fill the corporate coffers satisfactorily. The craze also spawned a Nintendo computer game, a cartoon TV series and a film which grossed thirty-five million pounds in its first five days (and was followed by two sequels). Throw in all the books, stuffed toys, key-rings, pencil cases, rubber balls and clothing and it adds up to worldwide sales of £3.8 billion.

With fighting rife in the playground many schools were moved to ban Pokémon cards and toys from the premises, which only confused parents who were using them as rewards for children getting good marks. 'It's difficult to know what to do,' said one dad. 'My daughter and her friends are totally caught up in this craze. I don't understand it at all and neither do any of the other parents I've spoken to.'

Packets of eleven Pokémon cards sold for about two pounds, but first-edition characters such as Charizard and Mew could fetch up to two hundred pounds in on-line auctions. Counterfeiting was rife and in 2000 US Customs officials seized fake cards worth fifteen million.

We use toys as an indicator of changing values, and in many ways they are. At the same time they provide proof of how little values really change. Despite all the silliest hype, it's silly to believe that human nature can be changed by marketing. Style and form may change, but the content is essentially the same. WCW wrestling figures are just the toy soldiers of 1900 moved on a century – except that now they boast Realscan technology, whatever that might be. Essentially the toy is still powered by a child's nimble fingers, a bit of aggro and a lot of imagination. Action Man is now as likely to be found on a BMX bike or roller-blades as in a jeep, but the way in which he is perilously manoeuvred into situations of extreme danger remains the same. Toy cars may now be Mitsubishis rather than Aston Martins, but they're still pushed along by kids who want to grow up and drive for real. Anakin Skywalker is simply the new Dan Dare.

Dolls are still here by the dozen, dressed in 2001's styles, of course, but basically with no more personality or reality than that which is invested in them by the child. No toy ever really comes into significance until it enters a child's imagination. Families still sit in the wreckage of wrapping paper and Christmas dinner playing whodunnits, howdoits and howthehelldyaplayits? Kiddies still impatiently explain the rules of games to their grans and grandads, just as Victorian kids no doubt were infuriated by their elders' failure to grasp the rules of Lotto. Monopoly, Cluedo, Scrabble, Connect4 and Frustration all still sell by the truckload. There's also the bizarre but perennial favourite Operation, in which gleeful kids remove various bones and organs from a plastic body:

'Operate Now!' invites the box lid. Mousetrap, one of the true classics, is still going strong after thirty-odd years. Gimmick versions of these games made brief appearances for double the price, but quickly vanished. Scrabbling for batteries to play Monopoly – whatever next?

Letter to Daniel

Fergal Keane

It is important in life to stand back and reflect on what we think is significant. In this short letter addressed to his newborn son, Fergal Keane, a highly successful journalist and BBC special correspondent, considers the changes that a baby has brought to his life. This reassessment of his priorities is mirrored by the changes that were taking place in Hong Kong at the time. As you read:

- *think about how the writer uses language to describe his thoughts and emotions at this special time.*

My dear son, it is six o'clock in the morning on the island of Hong Kong. You are asleep cradled in my left arm and I am learning the art of one-handed typing. Your mother, more tired yet more happy than I've ever known her, is sound asleep in the room next door and there is soft quiet in our apartment.

Since you've arrived, days have melted into night and back again and we are learning a new grammar, a long sentence whose punctuation marks are feeding and winding and nappy changing and these occasional moments of quiet.

When you're older we'll tell you that you were born in Britain's last Asian colony in the lunar year of the pig and that when we brought you home, the staff of our apartment block gathered to wish you well. "It's a boy, so lucky, so lucky. We Chinese love boys," they told us. One man said you were the first baby to be born in the block in the year of the pig. This, he told us, was good Feng Shui, in other words a positive sign for the building and everyone who lived there.

Naturally your mother and I were only too happy to believe that. We had wanted you and waited for you, imagined you and dreamed about you and now that you are here no dream can do justice to you. Outside the window, below us on the harbour, the ferries are ploughing back and forth to Kowloon. Millions are already up and moving about and the sun is slanting through the tower blocks and out on to the flat silver waters of the South China Sea. I can see the contrail of a jet over Lamma Island and, somewhere out there, the last stars flickering towards the other side of the world.

We have called you Daniel Patrick but I've been told by my Chinese friends that you should have a Chinese name as well and this glorious dawn sky makes me think we'll call you Son of the Eastern Star. So that later, when you and I are far from Asia, perhaps standing on a beach some evening, I can point at the sky and tell you of the Orient and the times and the people we knew there in the last years of the twentieth century.

Your coming has turned me upside down and inside out. So much that seemed essential to me has, in the past few days, taken on a different colour. Like many foreign correspondents I know, I have lived a life that, on occasion, has **veered*** close to the edge: war zones, natural disasters, darkness in all its shapes and forms.

In a world of insecurity and ambition and ego, it's easy to be drawn in, to take chances with our lives, to believe that what we do and what people say about us is reason enough to gamble with death. Now, looking at your sleeping face, inches away from me, listening to your occasional sigh and gurgle, I wonder how I could have ever thought glory and prizes and praise were sweeter than life.

***veered**: swerved

Snaps

Liz Jobey

What stories are told through the photographs we collect? In this piece, Liz Jobey tells several stories as she reflects on her family snaps. The family photographs, taken over the years, prompt the story of her parents' lives, her brother's and her own life. As she traces the story of her family through the photo album, Liz Jobey explores what photographs mean to us and what we use them for. As you read:

- *think about how Jobey enables the reader to imagine each photograph through the details she selects and the words she chooses.*

There is a photograph of my mother, taken on the beach at Robin Hood's Bay in Yorkshire when she was nineteen, during a holiday with girlfriends from her training college, that suggests to me something of how happy she must have been in those days – the days she talks about often now, since she's over eighty, and lives alone. Although she's totally **compos mentis***, I think those girlfriends are closer to her than the people she sees in Tesco and the greengrocers', and her neighbour from whom she maintains a polite distance. The photograph is of a young woman with an Eton crop wearing a backless

---

* **compos mentis**: sane

cotton sunsuit with a polka-dot halter neck that leaves her shoulders bare and divides into baggy shorts just above the knee. You can't see her face, because she's bent right over, hands on knees, head down, legs apart, braced for a person running in from the left of the frame to leapfrog over her. You can just see the hands and the feet of the person who's already in flight, preparing to land their hands on her back and jump – my mother is small, five-foot nothing (and shrinking, she'd say now), but what's so attractive about the photograph is how noticeably young and strong and smooth-skinned she is, and how physically active the photograph is as a whole. You know this person just out of the frame is going to catapult over my mother's sturdy frame in the next split second. On the back it says, 'Vicky was a bit early in taking this.'

I found the picture of my mother in the Black Magic box, still with its red satin ribbon, which for as long as I can remember has contained most of the photographs of our immediate family. There was a second, larger, shallower lilac-ribboned chocolate box where we kept the larger photographs, many of which documented the history of our farm, rather than our family: aerial pictures of the new pig shed, a particularly fine sow with her litter, the South Yorkshireman express steaming over the twenty-six-arch viaduct that crossed our fields, a new combine harvester, a clay-pigeon shoot. The Black Magic box was where we kept the smaller snapshots, some of them no more than three inches by two, of my mother and father with one or both of us as toddlers at the seaside, Yorkshire resorts such as Scarborough or Filey, my dad with his trousers rolled up, my mother with my brother poking in a rock pool with a scarf in her hair; or of my mother in her early twenties, sharply dressed in a striped blouse and knee-length skirt, sitting on a wall, one leg elegantly crossed over the other, swinging (as it were) a brown stack-heeled court shoe. The same shoes that, twenty years later, I would clunk dangerously around the house in, aged six or seven, wearing her old navy-blue nip-waisted suit, a pair of black-framed sunglasses with the lenses punched out, clutching a would-be clip-board, playing secretaries or, adapting the costume slightly, acting out one of the characters from my favourite series of books – *Jean Becomes an Air Hostess*; or *Susan Becomes a Nurse*.

Even at that age, getting out these two boxes made me feel slightly sick, and it still does. For years this complicated mixture of nostalgia and dread had a lot to do with the fact that I feared coming across an unexpected photograph of myself at my ugliest, around ten, with the short back and sides that succeeded the loss of the long, thick plait which had hung to my waist (and which I whisked out of the way with a toss of my head when putting on my raincoat weeks after it had been chopped off), the slightly protruding second teeth, the face composed of small plump cushions of fat placed one against the other into which my eyes seemed to disappear. Over time I destroyed any of these photographs as I found them, and now, when I discover any I had overlooked, I can still remember that feeling of a life doomed to unhappiness because of a bad case of puppy fat.

Most of these pictures were taken with my mother's early Kodak camera that opened up like an accordion with a delicate metal button on a stalk which you pushed to open the shutter.

In 1959 we took our first family holiday 'abroad'. We didn't go to France or Italy, places that were just being developed for tourism, but sailed – the arrangements courtesy of a friend of my father – in a boat to Eire, or what we called 'Southern Ireland'.

For some reason I remember more about this holiday than I do about any of those that followed, some far more luxurious and spectacular by comparison, and perhaps it was because I was small and it was the first proper holiday, apart from the seaside, in my memory. But also because it was photographed religiously by my brother, who not only had his new 35mm camera, but for the first time was photographing us in colour.

The writer Julian Barnes, describing his own family holidays in France when he was a teenager, said that it was hard, if he was honest, to know exactly how much of those holidays he remembered from the actual events, and how much he remembered because he had subsequently revisited those events through family snapshots. For a lot of people of my generation, the first beneficiaries of cheap colour printing technology, photographs constantly supplemented our recollections of real events. And usually they were the happy ones. Only professional photographers specialize in tragedies.

My brother was supposed to share the 35mm Kodak camera he had been given for his birthday that year with my father. The sharing part was because it had been such a lavish gift. In reality my brother was the one who had control of both the photographing and the developing. The films had to be sent off by post and they came back as transparencies, which in turn required a whole new apparatus for viewing. We had both a manual slide viewer, into which you slotted a slide and held it up to the light, and a slide projector and screen. From the age of seven to seventeen (when I went on my first holiday without my parents), these transparencies, which recorded summer holidays both successful and disastrous, were required viewing at least once, gathered round the projector in the sitting room to inspect ourselves on film.

Now when I look at these slides I scarcely recognize the people in the pictures. I can see facial similarities between myself and my mother when she was the age I am now. But trying to find signs in the child I was then of the person I am now, there is little to go on. My father and my mother look like two people coping with a family holiday. My father looks happier than my mother – he put family life at the top of his list of values. And my brother appears rarely. He was usually behind the lens.

For two or three years at the beginning of his teens my brother, **spasmodically*** methodical, catalogued all his transparencies in specially designed boxes, numbering

---

* **spasmodically**: occasionally

and captioning them; it was around the same time that he enjoyed collecting stamps, before all this grew boring.

Ireland 1959. We joined the boat at Liverpool: 'The docks', 'Family on boat', 'Docks', 'Sea loch', 'Floating crane' – all my brother's slides have a heavy emphasis on any sort of engineering or military installation. Then to 'Roche Point', 'Cobb', 'Black Rock Castle', me with dog ('Ardmore'), my mother with dog. My mother would have been just forty; she looks fine, slim, in trousers and suede jacket. My father, only in the earliest stages of corpulence; my brother already at senior school (I can tell by his socks with the yellow and black band and the green garter tabs) and all of us, the perfect family, healthy, innocent, together. No wonder, I think, looking at a photograph of my father and me, his hand resting lightly on my shoulder; my mother and me hugging a black dog here, a yellow dog there; the four of us, posing for the delayed action shot. No wonder we grew up thinking nothing bad was going to happen.

Like Julian Barnes, I'm not sure where my memory of photographs departs from my actual memory, but looking at these pictures for the first time in thirty years, I'm amused, even gratified, at the accuracy of my pictorial recall. Perhaps it's because these events were often discussed and became the stuff of our collective family legend: the day I paddled determinedly in the freezing Irish Sea in my navy-blue school gaberdine with breakers crashing behind me; the day I said *'Adios Amigos'* – as I'd heard cowboys say on *Hopalong Cassidy* on television – to the Spanish trawlermen at Bantry Bay; the horrible day I refused to kiss the Blarney Stone after making such a fuss about getting to Blarney Castle.

The events of that day are played out in a sequence of pictures which, in the expanse of grass surrounded by bushes, in the random distribution of the three figures in each of several frames – my mother, brother and an increasingly tearful me, and in the over-saturated colour, give an eerie atmosphere. I cried because my brother wouldn't let me have the ball we were playing with. I cried even more when I discovered that to get to the Blarney Stone meant hanging upside down, held by my ankles, and being lowered down head first to kiss the stone. I refused absolutely, despite complicated feelings of cowardice and disappointment, and despite my father's assurances that he wouldn't drop me. It had been the same with my first trip down a playground slide. 'All those other children are doing it, so why can't you?'

By today's standards, we were not a much photographed family. When I look at the total accumulated photographs from my immediate family, including the **meticulously*** catalogued sets of colour slides my brother took during his serious 35mm camera phase – that is, between the ages of ten and fifteen – they represent only a tiny fraction of the hundreds of sleeves of colour snapshots my friends collect of their children at every stage of their growing up, to say nothing of the camcorder tapes and videos of weddings and christenings and even mothers giving birth that they

---

* **meticulously**: carefully

seem to have collected over the years. I haven't yet been invited to watch someone's dying moments on film, but I can't believe it will be a taboo for much longer. Whether this exhaustive and mostly **banal**[1] documentation is, in the end, any more precious than the relatively few black-and-white snapshots most of us have salvaged from our parents' and grandparents' lives I don't know. There is a time when family photographs, and the past in general, becomes more precious to us than it has ever done before. Our parents die. We are the new **repositories**[2] of family history. We want to find out more about where we've come from, to make sure of the details, so we'll know more about why things turned out as they did.

For those growing up after the 1960s, family photographs serve another function. It is not only the technology of snapshot photography which has been radically altered, but the structure of family life. Families no longer live in the same towns and villages for generations; children move away from home. Wives and husbands separate; children are stretched between two estranged parents, sometimes losing touch with their grandparents altogether. Photographs, like the telephone and email, have replaced the network of the extended family. Photographs are how we keep in touch.

---

[1] **banal**: dull and ordinary
[2] **repositories**: people or books that have a lot of information about something

Sport

We spend an increasing amount of our time on sport, whether playing it or watching it live or on TV. In addition, the sheer range of sports taken up by people is also increasing. But why would anyone want to write or read about sport rather than play or watch it? The pieces in this section provide some answers. You can write about sport in all kinds of ways. Some writers seek to recreate the moment, to describe what it was like to have been there and seen something momentous. Some sports writers are themselves athletes and satisfy our curiosity to know what sport is like from the inside. There is investigative writing that researches questions and issues in the world of sport and autobiographical writing that seeks to explain a lifetime's passionate love or loathing of a sport. All of them draw us into the world of sport and help us think about the significance of what they describe.

Williams hits new high

Kevin Mitchell

In August 2004 the British boxer, Danny Williams, defeated Mike Tyson, the former heavyweight champion of the world. In this piece, the Observer *journalist, Kevin Mitchell, describes the occasion. The big fight is a classic subject for sports writers. Mitchell certainly conveys the drama of the event, but he also does something more which gains the interest of readers who are not boxing enthusiasts. As you read, think about:*

- *how the writer uses background details about Danny Williams and Mike Tyson to broaden the appeal of the piece*
- *how the details selected by the writer help us to empathise with the characters involved.*

Sunday August 1, 2004

Williams hits new high as he delivers knockout blow to Iron Mike's career

Kevin Mitchell in Louisville sees British 'no-hoper' confound the critics

The bad weather rolled through Louisville most of Friday, then a thunderclap to remember erupted shortly before midnight, the last of Danny Williams's sixteen unanswered blows on the ageing chin of Mike Tyson.

Down he went, draped and

dead-eyed among the ropes, near the end of the fourth round and down he stayed, to the amazement of a near-full Freedom Hall and viewers in 90 countries, most of whom were surely left to conclude that, after 19 years and a thousand heartaches, this was the last we have seen of Iron Mike in a boxing ring.

Far from the last, though, we have seen of Williams, dismissed here as a 9–1 outsider. Tyson started an unbackable 1–14 favourite. What fools Williams made of one-eyed experts and the bookmakers.

The quiet man from Brixton came to Kentucky, **derided**[1] as a soft touch, a fighter who has cried before fights, who is mentally weak and lacks heart. All of these barbs were thrown back at his critics in the performance of his career, one he might not match again, but one that he and all of us present will never forget. It was a fairy tale beyond imaginings – even though the fight came within half an hour of being cancelled because the rascally local promoter, Chris Webb, struggled to come up with his downpayment.

Oblivious to the drama, Williams went to the ring calm and determined. But he was all but out on his feet after a savage onslaught by Tyson in the first 40 seconds. He not only held on but then engaged in the sort of war of which few thought he was capable. Williams admitted that he abandoned his game plan of jabbing and moving after two left hooks had nearly separated him from his senses. 'Then', he said, 'I went to war.'

The intensity of the exchanges barely **waned**[2]. Tyson said that his left knee went on him at the end of the first and he complained that he could not get full purchase

---

[1] **derided**: mocked
[2] **waned**: lessened

on his left hook. It did not look that way either from 10 rows back or, I would wager, the couple of feet that separated Tyson and Williams for most of the short fight.

Referee Dennis Alfred, one of those clowns boxing occasionally throws up, ludicrously took two points off Williams in the third and later could not recall what for. Nor could he explain why he counted so slowly and distractedly over Tyson in the fourth. The lump of beaten fighter lay virtually motionless for 22 seconds, rising lamely only at the end of the count. 'I explained to them beforehand I would suspend any count if the other fighter was not in a neutral corner,' Alfred said. 'I stopped at six to tell Williams that, then resumed.'

Williams laughed at the explanation. 'The referee was a joker. Disgusting. He wanted to throw me out of that ring. He gave Mike every single opportunity.'

But Williams, one of the nicest people in a sometimes not-so-nice business, wanted to move on. He had made his point. This was a time for celebration, not recrimination.

His companion of 13 years, Zoe Browne, who hates to watch him work, turned up at ringside unannounced and, in the only logical conclusion to the magic, the winner proposed. They are, as he described it, 'Islamically married', but they will further confirm their bond publicly on 1 September, the anniversary of their meeting.

'I have never had a bigger moment than this,' Williams said, with sublime understatement. 'I always had the heart. I was sure of myself. I was relaxed and I was ready. I am going to chill out with my family [his daughters, Nubia, 5, and Maliha, seven weeks, are also here], look for a world-title shot or a rematch with Mike.'

The second option is unlikely. Tyson can now be officially rated a shot fighter and will be awfully hard to sell to all but the most desperate of **ghouls**[1]. He had three-and-a-half roaring rounds in him and every one of the 17,273 punters present (of whom maybe 13,000 paid) knew that the blizzard had blown itself out. Just as it had against Buster Douglas in 1990, Evander Holyfield twice and, most recently, against Lennox Lewis two years ago. There is nothing left.

We should not have been so stunned at the outcome, but we were – even those of us who had gingerly predicted that Williams would win – because Tyson, even in his ravaged latter days, retains a sliver of menace.

Two minutes and 51 seconds into the fourth round of what was supposed to be a routine engagement on his way to rehabilitation, however, the former two-time heavyweight champion of the world was reduced to the sort of **ignominious**[2] state he had been happy and able to impose on 44 of his 50 victims since he emerged from the Catskills in 1986.

Tyson, the youngest heavyweight champion at 20 and now the saddest ex-champ, made history and, cruelly, at 38 and £22 million in debt, with his earning power reduced from a projected $80m for a further four fights to zero, he is history. Freddy Roach, his wise and compassionate trainer, admitted as much. 'This definitely could be the end,' he said. 'No doubt about it. He said he was sorry he did not do what he was supposed to do tonight. I told him he did not have to say sorry. There are other ways to make money, even if it is hard to walk away from this game.

'We will sit down and talk, but money's not an issue. I am more concerned about his health. What good is money if you can't count it?'

The night belonged to

---

[1] **ghouls**: people who take pleasure in unpleasant or creepy things
[2] **ignominious**: humiliating

Williams, latterly of south London but soon to count the world as his home and his oyster. He was magnificent – and not only for dismantling a legend, but in his stout rejection of the slurs unfairly heaped upon him by people who barely know him and, it has to be said, did not want to know him. A Los Angeles writer referred to him as 'some guy called Danny Williams'. Others laughed at his chances, regarding him as no more than a foil. His was the deserved victory of a man who utterly believed in himself over a man who long since had even forgotten who he really was.

Tyson bought his friendship down the years, **squandering**[1] more than $300m in the process. Once destroyed, he lost his admirers. Sadly, he would probably have them back tomorrow if he had the funds. What happens to him now is problematic. He was saved the embarrassment of an **inquisition**[2] on Friday night when he was spirited away to a hospital for 'routine scans'.

There is no question that he underestimated his opponent. The build-up had been as subdued as anyone in the Tyson business could remember. No tantrums, face-offs or rants, no bad headlines or vibes. The strong suspicion was that Tyson was staying on his mood-calming medication until the last minute; Williams was just waiting, without chemical assistance, for the night.

But for all the real-life tragedies that **proliferate**[3] in the sport, boxing is essentially about pretence. Even the legends pretend. Even Ali. Few have identified boxing's most enduring myth

---

[1] **squandering**: wasting
[2] **inquisition**: a lot of searching questions
[3] **proliferate**: are widespread

for the **hokum**[1] it is – Ali throwing his Olympic gold medal into the Ohio river – as **astutely**[2] as the wizened New Jersey boxing writer Jerry Izenberg. 'If they trawled the Ohio for a thousand years,' he said, 'they'd more likely find a mermaid than an Olympic gold medal.'

From the crowd to the fighters, from the cheque-writers to the guys who get the beers in at home and cough up for pay-per-view, boxing is about pretending. Pretending it is as it used to be. Pretending we are in the same game as Dempsey, Louis, Ali and the rest. We are not. In the home town of the greatest actor boxing ever had, in Ali's backyard, we all put on our slap and acted up a storm.

Which is why Tyson, the creepiest of **parodies**[3], keeps getting the call from central casting. After a brief period on debut in 1985 as a man-child phenomenon, he has been playing the monster most of his working life.

His has been a spectacular fall, but no amount of examinations will adequately explain how he blew his career, and much of his life. To observe him at close quarters is to see a victim of self-loathing and overindulgence, a wild yet oddly perceptive individual with nowhere to go and no one to go there with. He lives alone in a borrowed room in Phoenix. There will be no more rising from the ashes for Tyson.

---

[1] **hokum**: nonsense
[2] **astutely**: cleverly
[3] **parodies**: people or things which have become exaggerated and ridiculous versions of themselves

Stealth the key to learning the art of fly fishing

Brian Clarke

How do you teach someone a sport or help them to improve? In this piece from The Times, the angling correspondent draws on his knowledge of fly fishing to write a short account for a 13 year old boy who had written to him for advice. As you read:

- *think about how well the writer explains the process of fly fishing. What techniques does he use to do this?*

Last season, I was fishing with one of my closest friends, a man who, because of his many excellent books and articles, has become a household name in the fly-fishing world. We fell to talking about the tide of angling literature – the thousands of books – that has been published since Dame Juliana Berners gave us the first work on angling in English in 1496.

My friend and I were as one. We agreed that while there had been works of technical brilliance over the years and many **sublimely*** written texts, vast numbers of books published of late had contributed only words. "They've just said nothing," I said. "In fact the really essential things about angling can be very simply stated. You should show everyone how. No, wait, I'll write a

---

***sublimely**: beautifully

new book myself. It will be called 'All You Really Need To Know About Fly Fishing'. And it will be about seven pages long."

My friend's stride faltered and his jaw dropped. "Blimey," he said, somehow conveying that his entire life was flashing before his eyes, "you can't do that – you'll put us all out of business."

It was a joke, of course, but for all that, the essentials of fly fishing would consume very few trees. Just before Christmas, I squeezed quite a few of them into a reply to the youngest Times reader to write to me so far – Peter Cox, 13, from Bristol.

Peter, who enjoys coarse fishing, wrote at his father's suggestion. On a trip to Wales, he had seen somebody catch a grayling on a dry fly and had been fascinated. What exactly was dry-fly fishing and how could he get started? Here, more or less, is what I told him.

Dry-fly fishing is a way of catching fish – mostly trout or grayling, but plenty of other species as well – on imitations of the kind of natural flies that they are accustomed to taking from the surface.

To do it, I told Peter, he would be best off with a fly-rod about 9ft long, rated what is called AFTM-6. He would need an AFTM-6, double-tapered, a floating flyline to use with it and a reel to put the line on. He should persuade his father to buy him a couple of lessons with a professional fly-casting instructor. The instructor would teach him how to cast correctly and practice would take care of distance and accuracy.

He would also be shown how to do fiddly things – such as joining a nylon leader to the line and a fly to the leader. He would be using only one fly at a time and it would be treated to float. At the water, the aim would be to get that fly to the surface in front of a targeted, rising fish in a natural way.

When Peter approached a river, I said, it should be in the knowledge that a fish is a wild and wary thing, easily "put down". What is more, he should know that in a river fish have to face the flow so, when they are hungry, they look upstream for the flies and bugs that the current brings downstream towards them.

What did all of this mean? It meant that he should avoid alerting the fish to his presence, either by the way he dressed or the way he moved, and that the best approach to a fish looking upstream was from downstream – from its blind side.

On the flies to be cast, I explained that most of the natural flies that fish eat are not much more than a centimetre long and that if Peter wanted to maximise his chances, his artificial flies should be tiny as well. This question of size, I wrote, was the single most important factor where artificial flies were concerned. The only

other important factor was colour and because most natural flies are drab as well as small, his flies needed to be drab also; browns and blacks worked best.

With these matters taken care of, the need was to ensure that the cast fly floated towards the fish as daintily and unhindered as the natural ones around it. That meant avoiding drag. Drag is what Peter would often see, after casting out: the current would push on the line and leader floating on the water and create a downstream curve in them. This curve would pull on the fly and cause it to skate across the surface in an unnatural way.

Minute amounts of drag, quite invisible from the banks, could be enough to kill all chances. Drag can best be avoided, I wrote, by having the minimum amount of line lying on the surface in the first place and by careful choice of the position from which the cast is made. Most often, the best place will be from just behind the fish and a little to one side of it; but often, paradoxically, it will be from directly opposite the quarry, as well.

When he had got everything right and his fish had tilted up, opened its mouth and taken his fly, I told Peter that he should give it a moment to close its mouth and tilt down again before lifting – not yanking – the rod end upwards and setting the hook. A few words about landing the fish, fishing barbless, the value of joining a local club and – well, all right then, the names of a couple of good books – rounded off the letter.

Peter replied by return, promising to do everything I had suggested and to let me know when his first fish was caught. I do not expect to wait long because he now knows where he is headed. I also know that, in my letter, I have the makings of chapter one – "All You Really Need to Know About Dry Fly Fishing" – in that seven-page book I had talked about.

Chapter two – "All You Really Need to Know About Wet Fly and Nymph Fishing" – surely cannot be far behind.

My friend will be appalled.

Mr Big rises to the bait in a small pond

Annalisa Barbieri

This first hand account by the angling correspondent of the Independent *paints a picture of fishing on a small quiet river in early summer. As you read:*

* *think about how the writer conveys the pleasure, drama and ordinariness of the occasion. What techniques does the writer use to make ordinary events memorable?*

Mr Big rises to the bait in a small pond

L ast Sunday morning, within fifteen minutes of smothering a warm and yielding croissant with gianduja spread, I was dipping a wadered toe in a river. Ah, there was that lovely familiar feeling: the water, always colder than you think it's going to be, hugging your legs tightly and squeezing all the air out of your waders.

I was in the River Box in Suffolk. There was a bridge behind me, a little weir some twenty feet ahead, a stable of horses to my left. In front of me a tiny, twinkling river, barely bigger than a stream, but full of promise. A big tree overhung it, the branches dipping into the water providing many a trap for my hook.

This wasn't a river that had been fished very much at all. Plus the fish were rising. What a great Sunday morning! Although this was the best pool – of maybe only two – my boyfriend, the generous soul, decided to **ghillie**[1] me while I fished.

The casting wasn't easy. I couldn't overhead cast because there were too many trees behind me. I reached for a black-ant fly, on a hook as small as a newborn's eyelash. I cast; once, twice, half a dozen times. We decided to change the fly. I say 'we', but in truth I'd have hammered away for longer with the same no-hope fly because I am so lazy. My boyfriend put a Tupp's Indispensable on for me as I stood in a semi-trance (nature does that to me).

The Tupp's was much easier to see on the water, too, which I like because fishing without being able to see the fly takes the edge off some of the banging-heart excitement.

Another difficulty was that the line caused slack as it came toward me, which meant that had a fish bitten I would have had little chance of tightening up in time to **render him set**[2]. But being over-enthusiastic risked dragging the fly and fooling no fish. Oh what simple dilemmas one has on a river.

Anyway, whatever I was doing must have been half-right because a fish bit. Now I always find when fishing a river for the first time that I need to 'tune in' to the fish's frequency and strike at just the right time, which is sometimes much slower than instinct tells you to do. I missed him, as I was to miss the next fish, too. But they were biting!

My heart was beating so fast as I watched my little fly

---

[1] **ghillie**: guide (in fishing)
[2] **render him set**: hook the fish securely

come toward me, knowing at any point a fish might fancy it. I got the next fish and the next. Then, I can't remember after how many but my boyfriend pointed to a particularly good spot beneath the tree.

I knew it was the most 'fishy' spot but I also knew that, because of that, it was the hardest to reach. Until this point I had been roll-casting, but now I had to cast sideways, shooting line between the water's surface and the lowest dip of the tree's branches. A big ripple broke just where we had thought there would be fish.

'That's a big fish,' my boyfriend whispered. I cast and, with a precision that I'd never shown in netball as Goal-Shoot, my fly landed at that exact spot. And Mr Big Fish rose again, this time to my fly.

'That's a big fish!' gasped my boyfriend again, slapping my back in pride as I played the fish in. We are, of course, talking relatively: the utterly wild brownie was about a foot long and lucky to be 1lb; but in these here parts that would make him 10–15 years old and very worthy of the name 'big'. What a privilege to meet him: he was beautiful with his lovely red spots.

With the greatest delicacy we unhooked him and he swam off. I fished for an exquisitely exciting seventy minutes more, while my daughter slept. I lost count of the wild brown trout I caught, and surrendered back, to the mightiest of tiny rivers.

Hating football

Andrew O'Hagan

Do you have to like football? And what happens if you don't when all your family are passionate about it? In this piece the novelist Andrew O' Hagan gives an entertaining account of how he survived as a football-hater growing up in a fanatical Celtic-supporting family and neighbourhood in Scotland. As you read, think about:

- *why this article has been included in a collection of writing about sport*
- *the techniques the writer uses to make this piece humorous and entertaining.*

I can tell you the exact moment when I decided to hate football for life. It was 11 June 1978 at 6.08 p.m. Scotland were playing Holland in the first stage of the World Cup Finals in Argentina. It happened to be the day of my tenth birthday party: my mother had to have the party after my actual birthday owing to a cock-up involving a cement-mixer and the police, but the party was called for that afternoon, and the cream of St Luke's Primary School turned up at 4 p.m., armed with Airfix battleships and enough £1 postal orders to keep me in sherbet dib-dabs for a month.

Things started to go badly the minute my father rolled into the square in a blue Bedford van. He came towards the house in the style of someone in no great mood for ice-cream and jelly, and within minutes, having scanned the television pages of the *Daily Record*, he threw the entire party out of the living room – Jaffa Cakes, Swizzle Sticks, cans of Tizer, the lot – all the better to settle down to a full 90 minutes with **Ally's Tartan Army**[1], now taking the field in Mendoza.

A full cast of Ayrshire Oompa-Loompas (myself at the head) was then marched upstairs to a requisitioned boxroom, where several rounds of pass-the-parcel proceeded without the aid of oxygen. I managed to eat an entire Swiss roll by myself and take part in several **sorties**[2] of kiss, cuddle or torture before losing my temper and marching to the top of the stairs. From there, looking through the bars, I could see the television and my father's face. Archie Gemmill, at 6.08, wearing a Scotland shirt with the number 15 on the back, puffed past three Dutch defenders and chipped the ball right over the goalie's head. The television was so surprised it nearly paid its own licence fee, and my father, well, let's just say he stood on the armchair and forgot he was once nearly an altar-boy at St Mary's.

My school chums were soon carried out of the house on stretchers, showing all the signs of a good time not had, by which point my mother was mortified and my father was getting all musical. 'We're here to show the world that

---

[1] **Ally's Tartan Army**: the Scottish football team
[2] **sorties**: rounds

we're gonnae do or die,' he sang unprophetically, 'coz England cannae dae it coz they didnae qualify.' My birthday was spoiled, and I decided always to hate football and to make my father pay. I had a hidden stash of books in a former breadbin upstairs – the revenge of the English swot! – and I went out to the swingpark to read one and to fantasise about becoming the West of Scotland's first international male netball champion.

Hating football was a real task round our way. For a start, my brothers were really good at it; the fireplace had a line of gold and silver strikers perched mid-kick on alabaster bases, and they turned out to be the only part of the fireplace where my father wouldn't flick his cigarette ash. For another thing, I went to a school where Mr Knocker, the teacher, was football-daft, and he'd sooner you packed in Communion than afternoon football. But Mark McDonald – my fellow cissy – and I broke his spirit after he gave us new yellow strips to try on. We **absconded*** from the training session and stretched the shirts over our knees, all the better to roll down Toad Hill in one round movement before dousing the shirts in the industrial swamp at the bottom. The destruction of footballing equipment was beyond the pale: we were too young for Barlinnie Prison, so we got banned to Home Economics instead and were soon the untouchable kings of eggs Mornay.

---

* **absconded**: escaped

My father gave up on me. Mr Knocker put me down for a hairdresser and a Protestant. But there was always my Uncle Peter, a die-hard Celtic supporter – not like my brothers, but a real Celtic supporter, the sort who thought Rangers fans should be sent to Australia on coffin ships, or made to work the North Sea oilrigs for no pay – and Uncle Peter for a while appointed himself the very man who would, as he delicately put it, 'get all that poofy shite oot his heid before it really does him some damage.'

Game on. But not for long. Uncle Peter arranged to take me to see Celtic and Rangers play at Hampden Park. He was not unkind and had put some planning into the day out, but not as much planning as I had: for a whole week it had been my business to make sure that the only clothes available for me to wear to the treat were blue. For the uninitiated, I should say that Celtic fans tend not to wear blue, especially not to the football, and *never*, in all the rules of heaven and earth, to a Rangers game.

My uncle was distressed. He called me a Blue Nose to my face (strong words for a bishop) and when we arrived at the ground he made me walk behind him. He said that if Rangers scored and I made a noise he would throw me to the Animals (the stand in Celtic Park where men peed and drank Bovril was affectionately known as the Jungle). When Celtic lost the game 1–0 he called me a **Jonah*** and said everything was lost with me and I should stick at school because I was bound to end up at university or worse.

***Jonah**: someone that brings bad luck

Easier said than done. Academic distinction at our secondary school was mostly a matter for the birds, so the best a boy could do was to set his mind on surviving four years of PE without ending up in the Funny Farm (Mrs Jess's remedial class, only marginally more humiliating than being excluded from the school team). It was a wonderful education in the intricacies of human nature. I had pals, good pals, and as a resident smoker at the corner and a fearless talker-back to the nuns, I was in a position to feel confident about their loyalty when we came before Mr Scullion, the chief lion at the gym hall.

Not a bit of it. No sooner had Scullion given some Kenny Dalglish-in-the-making the chance of picking a football team than all affection and loyalty would **fall away like snow off a dyke**[1]. First lesson: let nothing stand in the way of winning. My good-at-football **erstwhile**[2] mate would choose one loon after another – a bandy-legged chaser here, a cross-eyed soap-dodger there – until the teams were nearly complete, except for me and Mark McDonald and some poor dwarf called Scobie left glistening with shame on the touchline. A new deputy headmaster came to the school; you could tell by looking at his hair that he was all brown rice and liberal experiment, so I wrote him a well-spelled note about reversing the method used for the picking of teams. I remember the day and the very hour.

---

[1] **fall away like snow off a dyke**: disappear quickly (a Scottish expression)
[2] **erstwhile**: former

'O'Hagan,' the PE assistant said, 'pick your team.'

I walked the few yards onto the field like General Patton contemplating the sweep of his 3rd Army over France. 'Scobie,' I said, 'McDonald.' And so it went on until every lousy player in the group had smilingly succumbed to an early invitation from the worst football picker in the history of St Michael's Academy. My hand-picked Rovers and I got beat 12–0.

When I was 12, I had nearly run out of juice on the football-hating front; it was an exhausting business not playing the game. But then I had an idea of quite intense perversity. Even my friend Mark had to shake his head sadly and note that in the arsenal of anti-football weaponry my new device was just too much: for a moment he pitied my trophy-winning brothers, he truly felt for my Scotland-deluded dad. I had gone nuclear: Jacqueline Thompson's School of Ballet.

Ah, the pleasures of disownment. Before setting off to Dancewear in Glasgow to buy my first set of pumps, however, I was **dragooned**[1] by the seething Scullion to take part in a hateful five-a-side against Kilwinning Academy. What happened? With only two minutes to go I ran into the ball with the ferocity of a POW making a dash for the barbed wire. Reader, I broke my leg. As I fell to the ground in agony I was sure the *sylphides*[2] were coming to fetch me *en point*[3], but – after even more delusion – I woke

---

[1] **dragooned**: forced

[2] **sylphides**: magical characters in the ballet *Les Sylphides*

[3] **en point**: on the points of their toes, like ballet dancers

up in Kilmarnock Infirmary wearing a plaster cast the size of Siberia, and my father drove me home in perfect silence. The years have passed now, but I can still see him smiling in the audience many months later, the night of Jacqueline Thompson's Christmas Dance Display at the Civic Centre in Ayr, as his youngest son came onto the stage, football boots and socks pristine, whistle in mouth, to make his first appearance onstage in a dance number called – I swear to God – 'Match of the Day'.

Fit for life?

Diane Taylor

The athletes we watch at big sporting events are generally at their peak of physical fitness. But what happens to them in later life? Does the training keep them healthier than the rest of us? In this article from the Observer, *Diane Taylor interviews four former British Olympic athletes to discover how their fitness lasted. As you read:*

- *think about how the writer conveys the benefits and drawbacks of training to high levels.*

In a few days' time a succession of bodies **honed**[1] to the purest, most extreme form of physical perfection will run, jump and spin into action in Athens. The athletes competing in the 2004 Olympics have trained to a level unachievable for most people. The benefits are obvious – medals for the best, fame and admiration around the globe, and a **serotonin**[2] buzz without parallel.

But what of the downside? While medical experts universally agree about the health benefits of physical activity, there is an optimum level. Does the physical thrashing of the body at its peak leave it weak and

---

[1] **honed**: trained

[2] **serotonin**: a chemical released into the brain (especially after exercise) that causes happy feelings

mangled in the post-competition years or is it an investment that pays long-term dividends?

According to Dr Greg Whyte, director of science and research at the English Institute of Sport, the key to long-term health for Olympic athletes is not to cross the fine line between 'super physiology' and damage.

'Getting this right is dependent on how well the athlete is managed,' he says. 'There are a fair number who cross the line and this can result in unexplained under-performance syndrome, an ME-like condition that affects about 10% of elite athletes training in endurance sports.'

Osteopenia, a reduction in bone mineral density, is a condition that can cause long-term damage to both male and female athletes. It can lead to an increase in stress fractures although Whyte says that no one has yet proved a link with cause and effect of intensive training.

He and his team are studying exercise-induced asthma and looking at the impact of sports such as swimming and skiing where very high volumes of air go through the lungs on a prolonged basis. Environmental pollution absorbed into the lungs at much higher levels than that of non-competitive swimmers and skiers is thought to be a factor in the development of long-term asthma.

Anabolic steroids, which are, of course, banned but have been used by some athletes in recent years, can also cause long-term damage to the body, including early heart disease, increased tendon damage, liver disease and changes in the composition of blood cholesterol, increasing the risks of coronary artery disease.

Eating disorders are another occupational hazard for Olympic athletes. Research carried out at the University of Leeds found that almost one in ten of Britain's top female distance runners had some kind of eating disorder. In the short term, reducing body fat does improve athletic performance as oxygen can be transported to the muscles more quickly. However, in the longer term it can lead to the loss of muscle bulk as well as causing osteoporosis and kidney damage.

Managing Olympic athletes so that they can continue to raise the bar of achievement for the human body ever higher has become a highly sophisticated science. But the sheer complexity of the combination between genes, environment and training means that it is impossible to always achieve the ultimate super-physiology while at the same time insulating the body from long-term damage. Most elite athletes follow all the state-of-the-art advice available in the hope that they will not only win medals but also glide into an agile middle and old age. Then they unscientifically cross their fingers and hope for the best.

Christopher Dean, 46
With Jayne Torvill, gold for ice dancing in 1984, Sarajevo, and bronze in 1994, Lillehammer

Most of our training took place on the ice and we practised for about five hours a day. Jayne was my weights workout and I spent a lot of time lifting her. But it wasn't the conventional sort of weightlifting where you bend your knees – we always performed things off balance, which puts a lot of strain on the arms and on the lower back. Jayne used to hang off my neck quite a lot, too. Groin strains were common because of the stretches and extensions we were always doing. There was also a lot of mental stress associated with the Olympics. Everything you work for comes down to one routine of four minutes.

When we competed as amateurs in the Olympics we would practise all year for three or four events. When we turned professional, we did eight shows a week – at the weekend we did two shows back to back – with sixty lifts per show. We didn't work out how many miles we skated but at the end of each show we would have lost 2–3lb in fluids. The hardest thing would be having to perform even if we got a bug or food poisoning. After a performance I would look like the Michelin man with ice packs on both sides of my legs, on my lower back and on my neck.

We carried on performing together until five or six years ago. Now I choreograph shows for Stars on Ice. I have some arthritis in my knees and degenerative discs in my back because of the amount of lifting I did, but for a 46-year-old I'm OK. I've trained my body and my muscles to be a certain shape and if I maintain that, things aren't so bad. But after a hard day's choreographing, I tend to end up with the physiotherapist.

One of the great health benefits of spending lots of time on ice is that I've got fewer wrinkles than people who spend lots of time in the sun, like tennis players and golfers.

There was a sadistic pleasure in pushing my body to the pitch I did but I don't still hanker after that physical perfection; I've let loose now, I don't think it's healthy to stay that wound up for ever. These days I think that people who push their bodies to the ultimate goal have probably gone a bit too far and I don't think that's healthy. But I don't regret the way I pushed my body. Oh gosh, no. I wouldn't change a thing.

Colin Jackson, 37
Silver medal for the 110m hurdles in 1996, Atlanta

For my training as a sprinter I had to push my body by lifting weights and be as flexible as a gymnast, as well as the running. It was a total combination of work and I would have to spend at least four hours a day on it. It was hard when the weather was dark or gloomy but I could never miss a session because then I knew it would be easier to miss a second, third or fourth training session too.

I did push my body to its limits and because the body can only do certain things I had to train my mind to be stronger than my body. As a result, there were a few occasions when my commitment to training was too intense and my body couldn't handle it. At those times my body would literally crash and collapse. My knees have always been my biggest problem. I have had seven operations on them – one to realign the **patella*** and the

---

***patella**: kneecap

others because of cartilage problems. I've been told that the weaker the muscles around my knees become, the more chance I have of developing arthritis, so I have to keep them in shape if I want to avoid that.

At the moment there isn't any arthritis there and I'm not doing any running. It's way too much hard work to start that again. I did start training again with guys who are still competing but I started training too intensely – it's all or nothing for me. I've just come back from a skiing holiday and if I'm bored I'll do press-ups and sit-ups, but that's it at the moment.

I think that the most important thing any Olympic athlete can do to preserve their health long-term is to know when it's the right time to retire. If you want to retain your physical health, you have to know when to call it a day. I made sure I did everything I was supposed to do, which is why my career lasted for eighteen years. I really looked after myself and I had great medical backup. It's a legacy of those years that I can still do things like the splits.

Liz McColgan, 40
Silver medal for the 10,000m in 1988, Seoul

I used to train for about three and a half hours a day. I would run 145 miles a week for three weeks and on the fourth week I would have an easy week running 105 miles. I also went to the gym a couple of times a week, lifting weights and doing circuit training. These days I still run – I started when I was eleven, so it's a way of life. I just go out running once a day now rather than the two or three times a day I used to go out.

I think that, considering the amount of training I used to do, my body has done pretty well. I've got arthritis in my feet but so has my sister and she doesn't do much exercise so it's probably a genetic thing rather than caused by my running.

I did have one serious problem with my knee but that was a result of wearing ill-fitting **orthotics***. I've got a lot of energy as a result of all the exercise I do. I feel it's good to push your body to its limits. Every time I push my body further than I've pushed it before it makes me feel good. Seeing how far I could push myself is what gives me a thrill in running. I still time myself and I can still achieve the same highs I achieved during the Olympics.

Mary Peters, 65
Gold medal for the pentathlon (hurdles, shot, high jump, long jump and 200m) in 1972, Munich

I started competing at 16 and carried on until I was 35. I used to train for two hours a day because I was an amateur and athletics was just a hobby for me. With weightlifting, pentathlon, high jump, long jump and 200m, my body got a lot of abuse but I've just had my 65th birthday and am enjoying really good health. I've never

---

***orthotics**: special joint supports

been in hospital apart from one very minor thing overnight. I don't have any problems in my joints or anywhere else.

I would have 860lb weights on my shoulders and would do one-arm jerks with 120lb weights. I never warmed up properly the way athletes are taught to today, I never drank three litres of water the way people are advised today and I never ate pasta before an event as athletes are advised to do today. I used to eat steak and salad and I'm absolutely fine. I ran a gym for 20 years so I kept myself pretty fit and I've just been trekking in New Zealand to raise money for Mencap, walking 100 miles over the course of eight days.

When I was training for the Olympics I did work hard but it was just a hobby; it wasn't torture and I didn't push myself beyond my limits. I can remember one athlete saying that he was sick after every training session and that if he wasn't sick he hadn't trained properly. That didn't happen to me. These days, athletes do a lot of warming up and warming down but I just didn't have the time. I did pull a hamstring one season and I got tennis elbow early on because of poor technique in my shot-putting but that was all. I think the standard of Olympic athletes has improved enormously. I did it for fun and if I was successful that was a bonus.

I think physical activity has always been important in the evolution of men and women and I think people move around less than they did 50 years ago. Exercising makes me feel so much better mentally and physically.

I'm not quite as supple as I used to be but I'm lucky not to have suffered any ill effects from competing at Olympic level. I think it's partly down to genes; my brother is also fairly active and in good health. I feel as if I'm 18 even though I don't look it.

Holmes claims historic double

Duncan Mackay

Kelly Holmes was the first British woman to win two gold medals at the same Olympics. In this report of her victory in Athens, the Observer *journalist Duncan Mackay describes how it happened whilst also giving a sense of why her achievements were so significant in the history of British athletics. As you read:*

- *think about the details the writer selects to build a memorable picture of Kelly Holmes as an athlete.*

Sunday August 29, 2004

Holmes claims historic double

Sebastian Coe could not do it. Steve Ovett did not manage it. Steve Cram never even got close. But Kelly Holmes last night completed the greatest double in British athletics history when she added the Olympic 1500 metres gold medal to the 800m she won five days earlier.

She sprinted off the final bend to run herself into the record books by becoming the first Briton in 84 years to win both events at the same Olympics. Holmes joined Albert Hill, a First World War veteran and railway worker, who achieved a similar feat at the 1920 Antwerp Olympics.

The 34-year-old from Pembury, Kent, overcame blatant attempts by the three Russians in the race to gang up on her by pulling off another stunning triumph. They were clearly concerned about the potent double threat of Holmes's strength and speed. Natalya Yevdokimova appeared to have been told to take the race out as fast as she could in an effort to draw the sting out of Holmes.

The former army sergeant employed the tactics she used so successfully in the 800m on Monday when she beat Maria Mutola by dropping towards the back of the field. Yevdokimova ground out the laps in metronomic fashion with Holmes keeping a wary eye on any developments.

Even at the gun, reached in 2min 58sec, she was still in eighth place. Then she began picking off her opponents one by one. Finally, with about 60 metres remaining, and Yevdokimova trying to hang on at the front, Holmes moved into overdrive and there was a finality about it.

Holmes's body has been oozing power since she arrived here – from the muscular upper torso and **sinewy*** arms to the tiny hips and slim legs. But it never looked more powerful than last night.

Tatyana Tomashova, the Russian whose blistering finish was potentially Holmes's greatest threat, was powerless and looked across in despair as the Briton cruised past her.

The look of delight on Holmes's face as she crossed the line in 3min:57.90, breaking her own British record set seven years ago, was a joy to behold. This time

---

***sinewy**: long and muscular

there were no doubts. 'I just can't believe it,' she said. 'I'm gobsmacked.

'Obviously after the 800 it gave me so much confidence and going through the rounds I was feeling quite good.

'But the girls were so good in that race and I had to really focus mentally – probably more than any other one because I was tired and focusing was getting harder and harder. Now I can't wait for tonight to have a party.

'I was trying to place myself in the right position when I needed to and I was just focusing on where the leaders were. I realised they were pushing it hard so I had to move up. I was aware that if one of them made a break then I would have had it. So I just had to use all my guts and strength to hold on for dear life again when I could feel them coming.

'The whole experience has been absolutely amazing. I've trained so hard from when I've been out in Cyprus (at the British training camp) and

I've got so many people to thank.'

It is the nature of sport that fortunes can change quickly. But none has surely managed it as quickly as Holmes. Only a month ago in interviews she admitted the pressure was beginning to weigh so heavily on her she feared being crushed under it.

'I sometimes feel I'm falling apart,' she said. 'I feel this weight on me. I wake up worrying about the 1500m and go to bed worrying about it.

'I'm putting so much pressure on myself because it matters so much to me to succeed. But what can I do? How do you force yourself not to worry about pressure without just worrying more?'

Holmes's success in the 800m may have been a surprise, not least to herself, but she was already one of the favourites to win the longer race even before that brilliant triumph. After all, this is the distance she has been aiming for all season, and she only decided to enter the two-lap event last week.

Only two women have ever won both the 800m and 1500m titles at an Olympics, both Russians – Tatyana Kazankina in 1976 and Svetlana Masterkova twenty years later.

'I said she ran the perfect 800 on Monday and now she has followed it up with the perfect 1500,' said Coe, Holmes's hero who twice in 1980 and 1984 narrowly missed out on the middle-distance double by winning silver in the 800m and gold in the 1500m.

'She has hit a rich seam of form and she ran with great confidence and massive authority. She had the great advantage that, when it came to flat out speed, she could beat anybody. The others had to run away from her but she is so well conditioned they were never going to do that.'

Holmes is the first British woman to ever win two gold medals at the same Olympics. 'You have to recognise she has just made history,' said Coe. 'It has come at the right time for her. She would be the first to admit these will be her last Olympics and sometimes you need a situation like that to really focus the mind and confront what you want.'

Holmes has achieved her greatest ever triumph on the track that until these Games was the scene of her darkest moment. The last time she competed here at the world championships in 1997 Holmes arrived in the Greek capital as a huge favourite having just set a new British record.

It all went terribly wrong within three quarters of a lap of the opening heat when she pulled up injured with an Achilles injury. The name of the country that she once dared not mention is now her favourite destination.

The race

Cathy Freeman

What does it feel like to win an Olympic gold medal? How do you describe such an intense moment? In this piece, the Australian runner, Cathy Freeman, who won a gold medal in the Sydney Olympics, gives a vivid account of the 49.11 seconds which changed her life. As you read:

- *think about how the writer uses different lengths and types of sentence as well as powerful vocabulary to capture the moment.*

From the moment I entered the stadium it was there, a dull noise in the back of my head. It was weird. All I could focus on was my lane; I couldn't see or hear anything else. I started taking deep breaths to get as much oxygen into my lungs as possible. After a couple of run-throughs I discarded my tracksuit bottoms and long-sleeved T-shirt to reveal the swift suit. I pulled and prodded at the suit to get comfortable as I waited behind the blocks.

Just do what you know, Freeman.

My mouth was dry. I took a sip from my water bottle.

Breathe, Freeman. Breathe.

I arched my neck back to get another lungful of oxygen, licked my lips and waited for the introductions. I pulled the hood on, zipped it up and made sure that my hair felt comfortable.

Just do what you know.

From somewhere I heard my name read out so I clapped a couple of times above my head. The whistle sounded and we moved to the blocks. I got my legs into position and my fingers perfectly on the line. I stared down at the track and waited for the gun. The muffled beating in my head was gradually getting louder.

The sound of the gun blasted through me and I leapt from the blocks. I sprinted confidently around the bend and clicked into cruise control.

Relax, Freeman. Relax.

Graham and Merry had both started well on my inside. As the two-hundred-metre mark loomed I started to release the throttle.

Wait until the water jump, Freeman.

I held back on the bend and entered the straight a stride behind Graham and Merry. I couldn't believe how much I had left, and how conservative I had been in the biggest race of my life. With each stride the beating inside my head was getting louder.

Just keep moving, Freeman.

As I surged with eighty metres to go I sensed something was wrong. Not with me, with them. They weren't there. There was no pressure on my inside. I knew it. I knew from the start that none of these girls had the strength to go with me.

You've done it, Freeman.

Bang. It struck. The muffled noise was now a full-on roar and with fifty metres to go it vibrated through my whole body. The sound in my head had been the crowd. For the first time I heard them, I connected with them. I was floating. I felt like they were carrying me in their arms to the finish line.

The gap was five metres when I crossed the line. I looked at the clock and cringed: 49.11s. Slow!

Stop it, Freeman, you're now an Olympic gold medallist.

My body was numb. I removed the hood and bent over to take my spikes off. I had a sudden urge to sit down. I was overwhelmed with a sense of relief. It felt like I'd been trapped in a sauna and the door had suddenly been flung open. The fresh air was intoxicating. My God, I could actually relax. I felt like I wanted to cry but nothing happened. Ever since I was a little girl running around in Mackay I had dreamt of this moment, and each time I would burst into tears after crossing the line. My mind was whirling like a film reel locked on fast-forward. Images from my life were flashing by. Then, suddenly, they came to a stop. All I could see now was the beautiful smile of my sister Anne-Marie. She had been with me all the way.

Slowly, the enormity of what I'd just done started to sink in. *I'm just a little black girl who can run fast, and here I am sitting in the Olympic stadium, with one hundred and twelve thousand people screaming my name.*

How the hell did I get here?

I felt dizzy. I had to get the spikes off so I could feel the air between my toes. I could finally rest. The sense of expectation had nearly suffocated me. The pressure of knowing everyone was expecting me to win had been in my face every minute of my life for the past four years. Donna Fraser came over to me and I could see her big black lips moving but I couldn't hear anything. The pressure valve I had managed to keep closed was slowly releasing. I sensed the nervous energy of the crowd around me also releasing. I got up, took a couple of steps, and then it flooded over me again and I doubled over, closed my eyes and breathed heavily.

I did it! I goddamn did it!

Short cuts

Thomas Jones

Do you ever wonder where some sports come from? Who first thought of them? Or why? What are the origins of some of the equipment? Take pole-vaulting. In this short piece, Thomas Jones reflects on how, as a child, he was fascinated by this sport and speculates where it might have come from. At the end he turns to a different question – how high can you go? – to which there is a very precise answer. As you read:

* *think about what is striking and unusual about this writer's style.*

In the build-up to the 1984 Los Angeles Olympics, all the talk among the boys at my primary school was of Steve Ovett and Sebastian Coe. Clued-up children – in other words, those whose parents were more interested in athletics than mine – knew all about the rivalry between 'the Tough and the Toff', and because this was a posh primary school, the consensus was in support of Coe. Interest in him soon faded into the middle distance, however, as a new hero of the playground emerged: Daley Thompson the decathlete. Not just some 800-metre runner, here was a man who could apparently do almost anything: a true star of track and field (Steve Ovett dismissed the decathlon as 'nine Mickey Mouse events followed by a slow 1500 metres', but we were young and impressionable). What's more, Thompson got to do things that looked like they were a lot of fun: in particular, the pole-vault.

Part of pole-vaulting's appeal lay in its not being something we were able (or compelled) to do ourselves. A ditch and a line of trees ran along the edge of the playing fields, and those at the back of the queue for the long jump could (and would) leap the ditch with the aid of a stick: never mind that the ditch was fairly narrow, and using a stick was not only unnecessary but made it more likely that we would fail to clear the distance and fall in. Even at the time, we were all too aware – how could we not be – of the unleapable **chasm**[1] separating our efforts from the soaring flight of the champions: it was awesome, the way they launched themselves into the air in a graceful arc; seeming, for a still moment at the pinnacle of their **trajectory**[2], to balance on the end of the pole by a fingertip; before flexing over the bar and dropping the five metres and more back to earth.

The prehistory of pole-vaulting is, like that of many sports, murky. It wasn't on the programme at the Ancient Greek Olympics, though the Minoans may have used poles to leap over the bulls during bull-dancing events. According to one story, the modern sport derives from a traditional way of getting around the Fens of East Anglia, or other waterway-riddled parts of Europe, such as the

---

[1] **chasm**: gap

[2] **trajectory**: path (through the air)

Netherlands. At any rate, pole-vaulting was introduced to German gymnastic competitions in the latter part of the 18th century: perhaps in order to distinguish themselves from grubby peasants traversing canals, the amateur sportsmen concentrated on leaping not as far as possible along the ground, but as high as possible away from it. These pioneers used rigid poles made of ash; flexible bamboo poles were introduced around 1900, and the modern fibreglass variety was first used in 1956.

The notion that the sport might have had its origins in a form of siege warfare is appealing – Welsh hordes flinging themselves over the walls of Edward I's castles, pitchforks at the ready – but sadly without foundation: at the first modern Olympic Games, in Athens in 1896, William Hoyt of the USA claimed the gold medal for clearing 10'10" and he didn't have to carry any heavy weaponry. Even the crackest pole-vault assault squad, attacking a fortification with defences higher than 12 feet, would have knocked themselves out on the battlements. (Yes, Kevin Bacon pole-vaults to devastating effect in his battle against the giant worms terrorising the Arizona desert in *Tremors*, but that's only a movie.)

Today's top pole-vaulters can jump a lot higher than 12 feet (or four metres). It's fairly simple to work out the maximum possible vaulting height. An athlete running at 10 metres per second, with perfect technique and an ergonomically faultless pole, who converts all his kinetic energy (half his mass times the square of his velocity, or $\frac{1}{2}mv^2$) into potential energy (his mass times gravity times his height off the ground, or mgh), will be able to lift his centre of gravity 5.1 metres into the air (mgh = $\frac{1}{2}$ mv^2, h = v^2/2g, 10^2/9.8 x 2 = 5.1). Assuming his centre of gravity is a metre off the ground, he should be able to clear 6.1 metres. Which is slightly less than the world record, set by the Ukrainian Sergei Bubka in 1994, of 6.14 metres. Faster, taller athletes with better-designed poles might one day jump a little higher than that, but Bubka, whose record has remained unbeaten for a decade, vaulted pretty much as high as it is possible for a human being under his own propulsion to go.

Witnessing history

When something important happens, we all want to know the exact details – not just the facts, but also what people involved are feeling and thinking. Today we turn to journalists and broadcasters to bring events from around the world into our living room and to help us make sense of them. And we turn to historians or biographers to tell us about the past and why it still matters. The events described in the pieces in this section span several centuries and are told in different ways. Some are written during, or immediately after, the event, while details are still fresh in the writer's mind. Others are retold much later, after the writer has had time to reflect on the significance of the details recalled and the lasting impact of events. All, however, are eye-witness accounts, which means that we are more likely to trust what we read. One of the challenges for these writers is to balance their personal view of events, and their emotional reaction to them, with a more objective and generalised viewpoint that will be understood by a wide range of readers, many years later. As you read these pieces, think about how this balance is achieved. Look especially at the techniques used to describe events in a vivid and dramatic way that brings them to life again, and at how writers reflect on their experiences in a quieter, more detached manner.

Forgotten Voices of the Great War

Max Arthur

The First World War of 1914–18 still evokes powerful feelings because of the massive scale of the casualties. Its impact on a whole generation was felt throughout the country and in almost every family. We are all familiar with photographs of trench warfare, but what was it like to have been caught up in those events? To ensure that first-hand accounts of this experience were not lost, staff at the Imperial War Museum interviewed thousands of people who had served in the war, and created an extensive sound archive. In his book Forgotten Voices of the Great War, *Max Arthur draws on this archive to present a history of the war told in the words of ordinary people who fought in it. Their voices are remarkably direct, honest and matter-of-fact. As you read their accounts:*

- *think about how this direct style is created. What questions would you like to ask these people about their experience of war?*

Sergeant-Major Richard Tobin
Hood Battalion, Royal Naval Division

Colonel Freyberg said, 'Hello Tobin, how are you?' and I said, 'All right, sir.' He said, 'We'll get a **VC*** today,' so I

***VC**: Victoria Cross, a medal for bravery

replied, 'You can have mine as well.' He got his. Our final objective was the village of Beaucourt, but we hadn't sufficient men to take it so we dug in and waited for reinforcements to come up. The colonel sent me out on battle patrol. That's when you go ahead of your trench with just twenty or thirty men. You're there to hold up a counter-attack as long as you can. Well, that's a posh way of putting it. You're really there to do as much damage as you can, and to warn the front line while they're getting ready.

However, there was no counter-attack that night so we came back from our battle patrol all right. One of our men went out and came back in great glee. He'd seen a German wagon going along bringing their rations up, so he climbed over the back, **bayoneted**[1] the driver and pinched the mail. He brought it back to the line and that night we had **schnapps**[2]. In the mailbag was a box of cigars that had been coming up for the German commander, so Freyberg sent it back to our general. There was a jumping-off trench halfway across no man's land and the brigade was sent out to line this trench. We were assembled at one or two in the morning but then had to wait until quarter to six. We stood there in dead silence, you couldn't make a noise, and the fellow next to you felt like your best friend, you loved him, although you probably didn't know him a day before. They were both the longest and the shortest hours of my life. An **infantryman**[3] in the front line feels the coldest, deepest fear.

---

[1] **bayoneted**: stabbed with a bayonet (a knife attached to a rifle)
[2] **schnapps**: a German alcoholic drink
[3] **infantryman**: foot soldier

Then, it was just five minutes to go – then zero – and all hell let loose. There was our **barrage**[1], then the German barrage, and over the top we went. As soon as we got over the top the fear and the terror left us. You don't look, you see; you don't listen, you hear; your nose is filled with fumes and death and you taste the top of your mouth. You are one with your weapon, the **veneer**[2] of civilisation has dropped away and you see just a line of men and a blur of shells.

Then came the mist of dawn – a November dawn – and a burst of **shells**[3] which gave a dirty orange colour and left horrible fumes. We saw a gap in the line and closed in. Finally we reached the Germans' front line and saw some figures rising from the ground with their hands up.

Other Germans were still down their dugouts, so the bombers attended to them and we went on. We were soon across the second line and then the third, which was deserted, so we rested there a bit. I discovered my battalion was down to less than three hundred and out of twenty officers there was just one left – a captain. He was a very good chap, but he'd never been in a battle before. I was a sergeant-major so I knew what was to be done, but could I tell him, and could he do it if I did? It wasn't for me to do it, and I felt very lonely.

---

[1] **barrage**: shots fired from big guns

[2] **veneer**: thin layer

[3] **shells**: small bombs fired from big guns

Corporal Reginald Leonard Haine
1st Battalion, Honourable Artillery Company

I think Beaucourt was the most intense battle I was ever in, it was really grim. On the first day we had to get through the wire, which made a lot of casualties. Then there was a very complex trench system. And when you got through the first trench system you had a bit of open country and then there were these **redoubts**[1] and things that the Germans were holding on to. The Germans were very good at that time, they hadn't lost their nerve. And it was astounding to me that on the second day we did take Beaucourt, because we were very thin on the ground for that attack and the Germans had brought up reinforcements. I think, luckily for us, their reinforcements hadn't been on **the Somme**[2] before and they panicked. Otherwise we shouldn't have got through. The barrage put a curtain of shells over you, that was the theory, and you advanced. Of course you're bound to get casualties from your own shells, you were bound to get quite a lot of casualties when you were on a big show like that.

General Freyberg was wounded just near me on the second day. He stood out in the open and we said, 'For God's sake get in, Sir!' But he was like that and he paid the price; he went down. A chap who'd got about seventeen wound stripes over his arm.

---

[1] **redoubts**: temporary fortifications on a battle field
[2] **the Somme**: an area in France where many battles were fought in World War I

We had a most gruelling time that second day. When we got beyond the village and there were no trenches, we went into shell holes as deep as we could get. But they gave us the most almighty pasting that day with really big stuff. I think they were 11-inch **howitzers**[1], chiefly. It was a very grey day and you could see things coming towards you before they hit, it was a most unnerving experience. They came in **salvoes**[2] of four over. That was only one part of the shelling. Of course there were all the ordinary field guns and that sort of thing, but I particularly remember those big guns and seeing these little black balls getting bigger and bigger until they came in the most almighty roar round you.

After that show we were lugged out of the line for a while. Well, we'd got nobody left. I went in as a platoon sergeant on the first morning and within the first quarter of an hour we had our company commander killed and two out of three subalterns wounded, with the result that I became the second in command because there was nobody else left.

Artillery was the predominant thing in the later years of the war – the massed artillery. On one occasion when we were at Beaumont-Hamel in November 1916, we had a thousand guns massed on a mile front behind us. Well, you can imagine all this stuff coming over you, and with the German stuff coming the other way, you couldn't hear

---

[1] **howitzers**: a type of big gun
[2] **salvoes**: bursts of gunfire

a word. The noise of battle when you're out in the middle of it is so terrific that you can't hear any individual shots.

Corporal Clifford Lane
1st Battalion, Hertfordshire Regiment

The winter was so cold I felt like crying. I'd never felt like it before, not even under shellfire. What I had felt under shellfire, especially during the first two years, was a wish for a wound, a 'Blighty wound' we called them, to get me home. You thought a Blighty wound was the most fortunate thing that could happen to you.

But there were times, after being shelled for hours on end during the latter part of the Somme battle, that all I wanted was to be blown to bits. Because you knew that if you got wounded, they could never get you away, not under those conditions. You'd see other people with internal wounds and you thought your only hope was to get killed outright, your only relief. It wasn't only me who felt like that, it happened to lots of people.

I suppose we were **despondent*** because after two years the strain was terrific. The luckiest person in the war was the man who went out and the first day got a nice flesh wound that brought him home again. I've known men to be wounded three or four times soon after they'd got to

---

***despondent**: miserable and without hope

France. They'd go in the front line, be wounded, come home, go out again, be wounded again within a few days – the finest thing that could happen to you. If it was a slight wound you didn't suffer much and you were out of it. The worst cases were those who – and there were quite a few of us – went on and on, and on, without getting any relief at all.

But of course you had to take the chance of whether the wound would be a nice one or not, and there was a further danger of infection. A third of those wounded, even with fairly slight wounds, died of an infection. The soil in France and Flanders was absolutely contaminated. I was at Rouen hospital after I finally got my first wound and this old soul said, 'Yes, you've got a jolly nice wound there, mate, it'll get you to Blighty all right. But the only thing is, it's infected.'

Well I knew what that meant. I had a tube in here, and a tube in there, and every day the nurse had to take them out and start again. I was on my back for about six weeks, but it was the finest six weeks of my life because I could sleep and sleep and sleep. I had to lie on my back, but I really enjoyed it and the infection cleared up. That wound just about saved me I think – yes, it was a lovely wound.

Prisoners of war

Vera Brittain

When the First World War broke out in August 1914, Vera Brittain was 20 and preparing to go to university. But after only a short time there, she left and joined the Voluntary Aid Detachment (VAD), and assisted trained nursing staff in military and civilian hospitals, including those on the front line. During the course of the war, she lost her fiancé, her two closest friends and her brother, Edward. She wrote Testament of Youth *in their memory and it was published in 1933. Here, she recalls treating German prisoners of war in France. As you read:*

- *think about the challenges she faces and how she deals with them.*

Most of the prisoners were housed – if the word can be justified – in large marquees, but one hut was reserved for very serious cases. In August 1917 its occupants – the heritage of **Messines and the Yser**[1] – were soon to be replenished by the new battles in the **Salient**[2].

Although we still, I believe, congratulate ourselves on our impartial care of our prisoners, the marquees were

---

[1]**Messines and the Yser**: First World War battles
[2]**Salient**: an area surrounding Ypres where the front line stuck out into enemy territory

often damp, and the ward was under-staffed whenever there happened to be a **push**[1] – which seemed to be always – and the number of badly wounded and captured Germans became in consequence excessive. One of the things I like best to remember about the War is the nonchalance with which the sisters and the V.A.D.s in the German ward took for granted that it was they who must be overworked, rather than the prisoners neglected. At the time that I went there the ward staff had passed a self-denying **ordinance**[2] with regard to half days, and only took an hour or two off when the work temporarily slackened.

Before the War I had never been in Germany and had hardly met any Germans apart from the succession of German mistresses at St Monica's, every one of whom I had hated with a provincial schoolgirl's pitiless distaste for foreigners. So it was somewhat disconcerting to be pitch-forked, all alone – since V.A.D.s went on duty half an hour before Sisters – into the midst of thirty representatives of the nation which, as I had repeatedly been told, had committed unmentionable 'atrocities'. I didn't think I had really believed all those stories, but I wasn't quite sure. I half expected that one or two of the patients would get out of bed and try to attack me, but I soon discovered that none of them were in a position to attack anybody, or indeed to do anything but cling with stupendous exertion to a life in which the scales were already weighted heavily against them.

---

[1]**push**: attack
[2]**ordinance**: regulation or law

120

At least a third of the men were dying, their daily dressings were not a mere matter of changing huge wads of stained gauze and wool, but of stopping haemorrhages, replacing intestines and draining and re-inserting innumerable rubber tubes. Attached to the ward was a small theatre, in which acute operations were performed all day by a medical officer with a swarthy skin and a rolling brown eye; he could speak German, and before the War had been in charge, I was told, of a German hospital in some tropical region of South America. During the first two weeks, he and I and the easy-going Charge-Sister worked together pleasantly enough. I often wonder how we were able to drink tea and eat cake in the theatre – as we did all day at frequent intervals – in that **foetid*** stench, with the thermometer about 90 degrees in the shade, and the saturated dressings and yet more gruesome human remnants heaped on the floor. After the 'light medicals' that I had nursed in Malta, the German ward might justly have been described as a regular baptism of blood and pus.

While the operations went on I was usually left alone in the ward with the two German orderlies, Zeppel and Fritz, to dress as best I could the worst wounds that I had ever seen or imagined. 'I would have written yesterday … but I was much too busy,' runs a typical letter to my mother. 'I did not get off duty at all, and all afternoon and evening I

***foetid**: foul smelling

had the entire ward to myself, as Sister was in the operating theatre from 1.30 to 8.00; we had fifteen operations. Some of the things I have to do would make your hair stand on end!'

The desire for 'heaps to do and no time to think' that I had expressed at Devonshire House was certainly being fulfilled, though I still did think occasionally, and more especially, perhaps, when I was nursing the German officers, who seemed more bitterly conscious of their position as prisoners than the men. There were about half a dozen of these officers, separated by a green curtain from the rest of the ward, and I found their **punctilious**[1] manner of accepting my **ministrations**[2] disconcerting, long after I had grown accustomed to the other patients.

One tall, bearded captain would invariably stand to attention when I had re-bandaged his arm, click his spurred heels together, and bow with ceremonious **gravity**[3]. Another badly wounded boy – a Prussian lieutenant who was being transferred to England – held out an emaciated hand to me as he lay on the stretcher waiting to go, and murmured: 'I tank you, Sister.' After barely a second's hesitation I took the pale fingers in mine, thinking how ridiculous it was that I should be holding this man's hand in friendship when perhaps, only a week or two earlier, Edward up at Ypres had been doing his best

---

[1] **punctilious**: precise and formal
[2] **ministrations**: medical help
[3] **gravity**: seriousness

to kill him. The world was mad and we were all victims; that was the only way to look at it. These shattered, dying boys and I were paying alike for a situation that none of us had desired or done anything to bring about.

A Chinese square

Kate Adie

For many days in the early summer of 1989 thousands of protesters gathered peacefully in Tiananmen Square in the centre of Beijing to demand greater democracy and greater freedom from their government. The demonstration was seen live throughout the world on TV. At first the authorities were lenient but finally, on 4 June, the army was sent in to clear the square and thousands were massacred. Kate Adie was the BBC reporter who covered the event. This extract from her autobiography, The Kindness of Strangers, *is her account of what happened. As you read:*

- *think about the techniques she uses to recreate the chaos, confusion and violence of the night's events. How much of her own feelings does she reveal?*

The day passed and nothing **untoward*** happened. It was warm and muggy, and as usual we could gain no information whatsoever about official reactions from the leadership, which lives next to the imperial Forbidden City in a compound known as Zhong Nan Hai – a modern version of imperial **hauteur**[2], all high walls and secrecy. But towards the evening that Saturday, another column of soldiers had a much noisier confrontation with civilians at

[1]**untoward**: unusual or unexpected (in a negative sense)
[2]**hauteur**: arrogance

a flyover a mile from the square – and again, there were passers-by and bus drivers and old men on bicycles arguing with the military. All over Beijing – but unknown to most of us at the centre – similar scenes were played out for several hours, and any move the soldiers tried to make was blocked by swarms of angry citizens. We were out getting pictures all evening, conscious that the appearance of uniforms marked another step up the ladder of tension. However, the students in the square merely went deeper into discussion, and there were still sightseers and Chinese families wandering over the concrete expanse, revelling in the strangeness of it all. By this time, most of the foreign TV crews had headed for Tiananmen, including our American colleagues from NBC, who had two-way radios.

Just before midnight, I sat on railings at the edge of the square, nattering to a couple of students who spoke excellent English. They were both children of academics, and relatively sophisticated, gigglingly admitting to being boy- and girlfriend, asking shyly if it was rude to hold hands in public in Britain. They weren't sure where the demonstrations were leading – but they were sure that the country's new-found economic wealth had been grabbed by the inner circle of privileged party members, who had no **compunction*** about snaffling the best jobs on offer. They spoke with irritation of the relatively well-connected young people, sensing that unseen corruption might just

---

***compunction**: hesitation (caused by guilt)

impede[1] their own ambitions. They both dreaded the end of their studies, for the system was still operating that deployed graduates at the state's behest to work anywhere in the country, so they couldn't guarantee to stay in Beijing, or together. 'Are students in Britain ordered to different cities to work?' they asked. I wondered where to begin.

They perched on the railings, holding hands and dreaming, both smartly dressed and bathed in the strange tangerine-orange lights of the square. At that moment I got an odd feeling. I'm not overly superstitious, but occasionally there is the unmistakable **frisson**[2] of *something* – something which passes broodingly overhead, unseen but **emanating**[3] darkness.

At a quarter to midnight, I headed with the crew back to the Palace Hotel. A swish bit of chandeliered modernity, it lay a quarter of a mile back from Chang An, one of the main roads leading to Tiananmen, and we had our editing machines and extra phone lines there; we'd also bagged a few rooms in the gloomy Beijing Hotel which fronted Chang An, and had a view of the square from its balconies.

At seven minutes past midnight, I overheard an NBC radio crackle with the words, 'There's shooting, there's shooting at Fuxingmen.' I knew in my bones that this was no false alarm; it was as if a siren had sounded. Grabbing

---

[1] **impede**: obstruct
[2] **frisson**: shudder
[3] **emanating**: giving out

126

Bob Poole, our cameraman, and his sound recordist Alan Smith, we hurtled out, finding one of the drivers we'd used before who spoke a little English. We decided to avoid the main roads, and head for the location round the back of the Forbidden City. There was clearly something odd going on – hundreds of people were creeping out of their houses, pointing and shouting. Beijing at that time was usually silent at night; there was no 'night-life' and policemen discouraged any loitering.

We got our first sight of army trucks heading across the end of a small street, and we abandoned the car to walk down and join the little crowd watching a fire a hundred yards in the distance. Puzzled, we saw two of the crowd fall to the ground. There was consternation, with people bending over trying to lift them up. I couldn't figure out what was going on, for I was standing in the middle of the lane transfixed; an armoured personnel carrier had roared by, and a truck on the main road was on fire. There was thunderous noise, and petrol fumes and smoke. The fuel tank blew as I watched; when I looked back, I saw two **inert*** bodies being carried away helter-skelter. Only then did I realise the gunfire was continuous, and as we scuttled to the edge of the main road a truck went by with soldiers standing apparently ramrod-stiff. It took several seconds to realise that they were holding automatic weapons absolutely straight and hammering bullets relentlessly along the pavements and down all the side

---

***inert**: completely still

streets. We took a couple of shoots, and wondered how long we could stay in any one position. I looked in the distance up Chang An and saw scores of trucks and APCs heading towards us. A second truck went by – and swerved as something was hurled at it near the blazing vehicles. The soldiers went on firing. This is what an invading army looks like, I thought, shaking with helplessness. We raced away down the lane, past the small cottages which make up the traditional maze of housing, looking for our car. We spotted the driver, who was surrounded by a shouting crowd; seeing our camera, a man detached himself and pulled us into his cottage doorway. A tiny room, with every household article stacked neatly, a bare floor swept, and a blue-screened TV on a lace mat with an old-fashioned rabbit-ears aerial. On a low chair was a woman, a huge blossoming **peony*** of blood in her stomach, the bullet exit wound. The man was quiet, blinking, with a questioning look on his face. He crouched in the other chair, evidently trying to explain that they'd been watching together when ...

There was another commotion at the door; the driver asking if we could help. Outside a woman was being carried by her family – they wanted to know if we could take her to hospital. There was an air of panic as we tried to cram ourselves into the car and take her on the back seat with several relatives refusing to be left behind. Her skull was a mangle of brains and hair, though she was still alive.

***peony**: a flower (usually pink or red) with many petals

We careered down dark streets to the children's hospital; we found ourselves heading into hell.

Scores of people were jamming the entrance, all distraught, screaming, demented – and in a state of disbelief. In the twenty minutes we were there, forty casualties were brought in by bicycle, by rickshaw, carried in on a park bench. All the injuries were bullet wounds – in some cases multiple. There were elderly women, teenagers, children – not one seemed to be a student. We pushed our way into the operating theatre. It was a scene of mayhem, the living and the dead alike fetching up on tables, with the staff slinging corpses on to the floor. The whole floor was red with running blood. As well as panic, there was fear. Staff clutched at us, pointing to the camera and begging us to take pictures – but quickly. After a few minutes, two men erupted from another door and shrieked at us. The staff made it obvious that these were officials, and we were in trouble. I wanted to stay to get more evidence, but we legged it, for the atmosphere was wild, and the camera was precious.

We tried time and again to get near the square, eventually abandoning the car, and although I desperately wanted to see what was happening there, it began to dawn that the killing was taking place well away from Tiananmen. Ordinary citizens were being killed in their homes, the bullets ripping through the soft bricks. Onlookers, the curious, the disbelieving, and the frightened venturing out into the narrow lanes were being mown down. At one point I found myself between two men about three hundred

129

yards from the endless passage of army vehicles. The man on my right was crying and gripping my arm; on my left, the other man had a few words of English. As I turned to him, I felt the grip on my right arm slip – and at my feet was a silent heap, absolutely still.

At that point I wondered if we were going to survive. The odds seemed terrible, and still I felt that we had not got enough evidence of what was happening. I had a brief and halting conversation with Bob Poole:

'Should we stay out?'
'Course we should.'
'I agree.'

We both knew we had gone beyond the boundary of risk where we would normally call it a day. The Chinese army was killing indiscriminately with powerful weapons, and added to that, the secret police and other officials were hunting for foreign journalists: in the hospital, and also when approaching groups of onlookers, we had seen people scatter as anonymous men barked at them and then turned to head for us. However, one of my worries at that point was that after over two and a half hours on the streets, we had seen just one other member of the media – a Canadian cameraman. For the majority of the press, I later learned, were still gathered in the square – or, like my own colleagues, had stayed in the Beijing Hotel to watch events from the balcony.

From the hospital, I managed to call the office and alert

them to the scale of events and made clear our intention of staying with the story for as long as possible.

'It's appalling, it's dreadful', I said, for the first time having to find words, however inadequate, to describe what we were seeing.

And still the troops came in – and now tanks: the 38th Army and the 27th, tough professionals, who nevertheless managed to shoot each other in a major cock-up in the suburbs, and whose orders, it's now believed, were unclear and wrongly executed. Be that as it may, the force now let loose on the streets was a body of men completely ignorant of the situation in Tiananmen, fed the line that they were on their way to 'put down a rebellion' which was led by 'counter-revolutionary thugs' – and with every intention of shooting their way to victory.

Along Chang An, we could see signs of resistance – stones littered the road, and the number of vehicles on fire growing. As we finally made our way to the edge of the square, having taken a roundabout route on foot, we were having problems with students calling attention to our camera. They were so desperate, they clung to us and shouted to their mates and tried to drag us this way and that, to show us another body, or a wrecked vehicle. This only made us more vulnerable, drawing attention to the camera and alerting the creepy secret police; but we were eventually lucky.

A pony-tailed man who said he was called Li attached himself to us and proved a marvellous friend. He was too old to be a student, and had a dark, characterful face; he spoke a little English and instantly understood the problem, shushing the students, and guiding us nimbly through back alleys and courtyards. I put my faith in him – and prayed that he wasn't a secret policeman. Instead, he got us to the edge of the square, which by 3a.m. was partially under the control of the army, though we could see only lines of troops blocking our access. There were still thousands of students standing defiantly, confronting the soldiers, and as we walked nearer I realised they were singing **the Internationale**[1].

As they sang, there was a tremendous roar of gunfire, which lasted for minutes, starting a stampede, with bicycles and rickshaws intermingled. Li pointed to the far side of the boulevard – and we dashed across a couple of hundred yards while people fell around us. In the shadow of a government building, we lay on the ground and considered our options. We were breathless and bewildered and outraged. I knew that I had to get on a phone to London for the main news bulletin, and that there was only an hour or so before the deadline; I felt it **imperative**[2] to deliver an eyewitness report, for clearly the killing was going to continue, and such action should be exposed as soon as possible.

The crowd soon reformed in front of the soldiers and we risked a 'stand-up', just a few seconds of me talking to the camera – but we were interrupted four times by immense

---

[1]**the Internationale**: the international communist anthem
***imperative**: urgently necessary

volleys and rushing students. Over an hour later, we got a take, having witnessed ambulance drivers being injured and white-coated medical staff being shot. I decided to head back to the hotel with the one precious cassette, for I was getting worried that if we lost it to some soldier, the whole night's work would have been in vain. Bob and Alan opted to stay **in the lee of*** the building, because it was obvious that the only way back to the hotel was across a long expanse of open ground, running parallel to the soldiers' line.

I set off at a hard run and had gone only fifty yards when the firing began again. There was chaos, hundreds of people were blundering in all directions. My arm flipped upwards and lost the cassette, and simultaneously a young man cannoned into me. I went full length over him and lay with my face on the tarmac, watching little scarlet ticks flashing on the ground just a yard away. I had no notion that they were bullets. I crawled after the cassette, and turned to apologise to the young man. He had a huge seeping hole in his back – and I had blood running down my arm. The bullet which took a nick out of my elbow had killed him.

I set off again, possessed with fear and rage. I ran towards the Beijing Hotel just beyond the edge of the square, hoping the BBC was somewhere in the rooms we'd rented. A safe haven, I was squeaking to myself, and then found the gates fastened shut with wire.

***in the lee of**: next to

Bugger that, I thought, and, like an animal, went for the wall.

I got up it in one go, clawing at the stone, and only when I got to the top did I realise it was at least eight feet high. I half slid down the other side, too chicken to jump, and trotted across the compound, which was eerily silent, clutching the tape. The lobby looked dimly lit – too late, I saw three policemen inside. Also coming across the lobby were two Chinese, shouting as the glass door was pushed open: 'Run for it – they'll arrest you!' By then I was halfway through, and mad.

A policeman went for the tape in my hand. I kicked him in the groin, punched the second with my left hand, and body-charged the third. I'm no fighter, but surprise and a sense of outrage are enough. I then hurtled to the stairs, with the two strangers shouting 'Go for it!' as they deliberately got in the way of the cops. I streaked up the stairs – realising I had no idea on which floor we had our office. I tried two floors, hammering on doors, until I struck lucky, cannoning in on *Newsnight*'s Julian O'Halloran. I looked a complete fright, blood and grit everywhere, and with my fingers locked so rigidly round the cassette it had to be prised free, but I was staggered to find the entire BBC operation hotel-bound, viewing the carnage from the balcony.

I mustered everything I could to find the right words, the words which would both paint a picture accurately and convey a sense of the scale and the atmosphere – for we could not send TV pictures directly: all we had was a telephone line.

After such a night, there should have been some respite, but neither the Chinese army nor the protesters had given up. Even though the streets had quietened down, and the students had been marshalled from the square under army guard a short time after I had left, with Bob and Alan making it safely back, the next few days saw a city in defiant mood. There were frequent bursts of gunfire – so much so that it became the norm like Beirut in wartime.

Disaster

John Simpson

Writing first hand about war is difficult. There are so many things happening, often across vast areas. There are restrictions on what can be said and the outcome of the conflict is uncertain. And it's dangerous. John Simpson has reported on Iraq for 20 years for the BBC. In this extract from The Wars Against Saddam, *he tells of an incident when American F-14 aircraft bombed by mistake a convoy in which he was travelling. One of the camera crew died and several, including Simpson himself, were injured. As you read:*

- *think about how Simpson carefully pieces together events leading up to the attack. What details does he include and why?*

It was eerie. The road was entirely empty, and we had no clear knowledge of what might lie ahead – just someone's assertion that **Dibarjan*** had fallen. There were occasional loud explosions coming from somewhere, but it was hard to know where. Our car was in the lead, and Fred and I were becoming less and less certain about carrying on. The driver, sensing our feelings, slowed down; at that moment there was a roar of engines behind us in the distance, and a cloud of dust. Instinctively, our driver pulled over to the side of the road.

*__*Dibarjan__: a town in northern Iraq

There must have been sixteen of them: big Land Cruisers, new and still quite shiny. The first couple bore big **KDP**[1] flags, and after the Kurdish part of the convoy had passed there were several American vehicles with big Stars and Stripes carrying special forces soldiers.

'It's Waji,' said Kamaran.

Waji Barzani was an impressive character: the younger brother of the KDP president, and the leader of the **Pesh Merga**[2]'s special forces. We had interviewed him a couple of days before. This was a very high-level group indeed, and it would be excellent for us to stick with them. Our driver slotted in behind them on the road. The dust welled up all round us. At one point we stopped. The Iraqis had dug mines into the road, and we had to make a wide detour over a muddy hillside to get past them. A couple of American planes were circling overhead, I noticed.

Ahead of us lay a ridge, and the Kurdish and American vehicles were stopping there.

'**Flak-jacket**[3] time,' I said.

At times like these, the speed with which you do things can change everything. If we had taken more time to catch up, or if we had stayed a little longer in our cars, we would have burned to death as so many of the other people around us would shortly do. They, and Kamaran, had only a few minutes of life left.

---

[1] **KDP**: Kurdish Democratic Party of Iraq

[2] **Pesh Merga**: the Kurdish militia in Iraq

[3] **Flak-jacket**: a bullet proof jacket or vest

The convoy had stopped at a crossroads on the top of a hill, and Waji Barzani and his men were standing there looking down into the valley beyond, in the direction of Dibarjan. Someone was pointing towards a couple of Iraqi tanks about a mile away in the valley below us, and I realized then that the thin column of black smoke which was still hanging in the air a few hundred yards behind us had come from a shell fired by one of the tanks. The American special forces vehicles were drawn up alongside each other close by, each flying a gigantic Stars and Stripes. A little ahead of us, down the road, several American armoured personnel carriers had also stopped. They too carried vast flags.

The rest of the vehicles in the convoy, a dozen or so of them, all displayed big panels of orange material on their roofs, clearly visible from the air. Our vehicles had them too. In other words, if you were a pilot flying reasonably low you could not have glanced at the scene on the ground and mistaken us for the enemy. I heard the sound of a radio crackling; one of the Americans was calling an air strike against the tanks. By chance, there was a wrecked Iraqi tank lying right beside the crossroads; it must have been attacked and destroyed earlier in the day. It's not impossible that the presence of this tank, when an attack was being requested on another tank nearby, caused the disaster that followed.

The two US Navy F-14s were flying very low; about 1,000 feet. Fred Scott wanted to film them as we were standing near the group around Waji Barzani, and called out to Tom Giles that he needed his tripod to film the planes.

'OK – tripod,' I heard Tom shout back. He and Craig headed off back to our vehicles.

I was aware of Fred standing quite close to me, and Kamaran about six feet away. Dragan was also there somewhere: he said something too, which I couldn't hear. The noise of the planes overhead was too loud.

Just as Tom was getting the tripod out of the vehicle, his phone rang. It was his birthday, and his mother was calling to wish him many happy returns. He thanked her, then held the phone up in the air so she could hear the noise the planes were making.

'Listen, Mum, that's the sound of freedom,' he said, to tease her; she was strongly against war.

As she listened, there was a huge whistling roar at the other end of the phone, followed by a terrible explosion. For an instant she must have thought Tom was dead, but then she heard his voice swearing. He had forgotten she was there, and was blundering around in the smoke that was rising from the centre of the crossroads, still holding the phone. Car alarms were starting to go off, and all round there were the screams and groans of injured and dying men.

Twenty yards away, on the other side of the parked cars, Fred and I both saw the bomb as it landed. I found it hard afterwards to credit my senses, but when I checked what I had seen with Fred I realized it was true. There was an immense downward force, hitting the ground at an acute

139

angle, and I had the impression of something white and red. Late in 2003, Tom Giles and I were given a reluctant briefing by the Pentagon about the attack. We were told it had been a 1,000-lb bomb which had been dropped on us. The angle of the detonation was so acute that anyone standing outside the vector of its blast, as we were, had a chance of surviving. Most of my team and I were between ten and twelve yards away.

Fourteen pieces of shrapnel hit me altogether, and I was knocked to the ground. Most were pretty small, like the ones that hit me in the face and head, but two the size of bullets were enough to have killed me. One lodged in my left hip, the other stuck in the plastic plate of my flak-jacket over the spine. I was wearing a pair of those trousers that unzip to turn into shorts; the left leg section was entirely blasted off its zip by the explosion, leaving my leg naked and bleeding.

I lost consciousness for an instant, then felt myself being pulled up. Dragan, instead of running for shelter, had come back to help me, thinking that the plane might drop a second bomb on us. People have won medals for less bravery than he showed. He ran across the grass, pulling me along by the wrist, so fast that I fell over again.

'Leave me alone,' I shouted at him; it was scarcely gracious.

He and I stumbled across the grass, and it was only later that I remembered what had happened to **Kaveh Golestan***

****Kaveh Golestan**: a BBC cameraman who died when he stepped on a landmine in Iraq in 2003

and realized we had already come across a line of mines across the road half a mile back. Fortunately, no one had laid any mines here.

The fire of London

Samuel Pepys

The Great Fire of London broke out on the night of 2 September 1666 and raged for four days and nights. It caused more damage than any similar disaster until the blitz of 1940–41. Few lives were lost but some four-fifths of the total area of the city was destroyed. Many records of the time refer to the fire but our knowledge of what it was really like is largely due to one man, Samuel Pepys. He was a naval administrator and for many years kept a detailed diary of his life in London. This is his account of the fire. As you read:

- *think about the way Pepys mixes together details of his domestic life, his feelings about the fire, and objective facts about the destruction caused.*

2 September, Lords Day. Some of our maids sitting up late last night to get things ready against our feast today, Jane called us up, about 3 in the morning, to tell us of a great fire they saw in the City. So I rose, and slipped on my nightgown and went to her window, and thought it to be on the back side of Markelane at the furthest; but being unused to such fires as followed, I thought it far enough off, and so went to bed again and to sleep. About 7 rose again to dress myself, and there looked out at

the window and saw the fire not so much as it was, and further off. So to my closet to set things to rights after yesterday's cleaning. By and by Jane comes and tells me that she hears that above 300 houses have been burned down tonight by the fire we saw, and that it was now burning down all Fishstreet by London Bridge. So I made myself ready presently, and walked to the Tower and there got upon one of the high places, Sir J. Robinsons little son going up with me; and there I did see the houses at that end of the bridge all on fire, and an infinite great fire on this and the other side the end of the bridge – which, among other people, did trouble me for poor little Michell and our Sarah on the Bridge. So down, with my heart full of trouble, to the Lieutenant of the Tower, who tells me that it begun this morning in the King's bakers house in Pudding Lane, and that it hath burned down St Magnes Church and most of Fishstreete already. So I down to the waterside and there got a boat [to the] bridge, and there saw a lamentable fire. Poor Michells house, as far as the Old Swan, already burned that way and the fire running further, that in a very little time it got as far as the Scillyard while I was there. Everybody **endeavouring*** to remove their goods, and flinging into

---

* **endeavouring**: trying hard

143

the river or bringing them to **lighters**[1] that lay off
[the banks]. Poor people staying in their houses as
long as till the very fire touched them, and then
running into boats or clambering from one pair of
stair[s] by the waterside to another. And among other
things, the poor pigeons I perceive were **loath**[2] to
leave their houses, but hovered about the windows and
balconies till they were some of them burned, their
wings, and fell down.

Having stayed, and in an hour's time seen the fire
rage every way, and nobody to my sight endeavouring
to **quench**[3] it, but to remove their goods and leave all
to the fire; and having seen it get as far as the
Steeleyard, and the wind mighty high and driving it
into the city, and everything, after so long a drought,
proving **combustible**[4], even the very stones of the
churches. I – with a gentleman with me who desired
to go off from the Tower to see the fire in my boat
– to Whitehall, and there to the King's closet in the
chapel, where people came about me and I did give
them an account [that] dismayed them all; and word
was carried to the King, so I was called and did tell

---

[1] **lighters**: river boats used for unloading big ships
[2] **loath**: reluctant
[3] **quench**: put out
[4] **combustible**: flammable

144

the King and Duke of York what I saw, and that
unless his Majesty did command houses to be pulled
down, nothing could stop the fire. They seemed much
troubled, and the King commanded me to go to my Lord
Mayor from him and command him to spare no houses
but to pull [them down] before the fire every way.
The Duke of York bid me tell him that if he would
have any more soldiers, he shall. I in his coach to
St. Pauls Cathedral; and there walked along Watling
Street as well as I could, every creature coming away
loaden with goods to save — and here and there sick
people carried away in beds. Extraordinary good goods
carried in carts and on backs. At last met my Lord
Mayor in Canning Streete, like a man spent, with
hankercher about his neck. To the King's message, he
cried like a fainting woman, 'Lord, what can I do? I
am spent! People will not obey me. I have been
pull[ing] down houses. But the fire overtakes us
faster than we can do it.' That he needed more
soldiers; and that for himself, he must go and refresh
himself, having been up all night. So he left me, and
I him, and walked home — seeing people all almost
distracted and no manner of means used to quench
the fire. The houses too, so very thick hereabouts,
and full of matter for burning, as pitch and tar, in
Thames street — and warehouses of oyle and wines
and brandy and things. And to see the churches all

145

filling with goods, by people who themselves should have been quietly there at this time.

As soon as dined, I and Moore away and walked through the City, the streets full of nothing but people and horses and carts loaden with goods, ready to run over one another, and removing goods from one burned house to another — they now removing out of Canning Street (which received goods in the morning) into Lumbard Streete and further. We parted at St. Pauls, he home and I to Pauls Wharf, where I had appointed a boat to attend me; and took in Mr Carcasse and his brother, whom I met in the street, and carried them below and above bridge, to and again, to see the fire, which was now got further, both below and above, and no likelihood of stopping it. Met with the King and Duke of York in their barge. Their order was to pull down houses apace*, and so below bridge at the waterside; but little was or could be done, the fire coming upon them so fast. Good hopes there was of stopping it at the Three Cranes above, and at Buttolphs Wharf below bridge, if care be used; but the wind carries into the City, so as we know not by the waterside what it doth there. River full of lighter[s] and boats taking in goods, and

---

*apace: quickly

good goods swimming in the water. Having seen as much as I could now, I away to Whitehall by appointment, and there walked to St James's Park, and there met my wife and Creed and Wood and his wife and walked to my boat, and there upon the water again, and to the fire up and down, it still increasing and the wind great. So near the fire as we could for smoke; and all over the Thames, with one's face in the wind you were almost burned with a shower of firedrops — this is very true — so as houses were burned by these drops and flakes of fire, three or four, nay five or six houses, one from another. When we could endure no more upon the water, we to a little alehouse on the Bankside above the Three Cranes, and there stayed till it was dark almost and saw the fire grow; and as it grow darker, appeared more and more, and in corners and upon steeples and between churches and houses, as far as we could see up the hill of the City, in a most horrid malicious bloody flame, not like the fine flame of an ordinary fire. We stayed till, it being darkish, we saw the fire as only one entire arch of fire from this to the other side the bridge, and in a bow up the hill, for an arch of above a mile long. It made me weep to see it. The churches, houses, and all on fire and flaming at once, and a horrid noise the flames made, and the cracking of houses at their ruine.

The story of an eyewitness

Jack London

In 1906 much less was known about earthquakes and their causes than it is today. In that year, the booming city of San Francisco was devastated by an earthquake which was followed by extensive fires. The shock of the event travelled rapidly through America and Collier's magazine commissioned the novelist, Jack London, who lived near the city, to go there to write the story of what he saw. As you read:

- *think about how the author uses contrasts to add impact to the report. In particular look at the way that contrasts are shown between the power of nature and the powerlessness of man, and between calm and chaos in the city.*

May 5, 1906

THE STORY OF AN EYEWITNESS

By Jack London, *Collier's* special correspondent

The earthquake shook down in San Francisco hundreds of thousands of dollars' worth of walls and chimneys. But the **conflagration*** that followed

---

***conflagration**: large and destructive fire

burned up hundreds of millions of dollars' worth of property. There is no estimating within hundreds of millions the actual damage wrought. Not in history has a modern imperial city been so completely destroyed. San Francisco is gone. Nothing remains of it but memories and a fringe of dwelling-houses on its outskirts. Its industrial section is wiped out. Its business section is wiped out. Its social and residential section is wiped out. The factories and warehouses, the great stores and newspaper buildings, the hotels and the palaces of the **nabobs**[1], are all gone. Remains only the fringe of dwelling houses on the outskirts of what was once San Francisco.

Within an hour after the earthquake shock the smoke of San Francisco's burning was a **lurid**[2] tower visible a hundred miles away. And for three days and nights this lurid tower swayed in the sky, reddening the sun, darkening the day, and filling the land with smoke.

On Wednesday morning at a quarter past five came the earthquake. A minute later the flames were leaping upward. In a dozen different quarters south of Market Street, in the working-class ghetto, and in the factories, fires started. There was no opposing the flames. There was no organization, no communication. All the cunning adjustments of a twentieth century city had been smashed by the earthquake. The streets were humped into ridges and depressions, and piled with the debris of fallen walls. The steel rails were twisted into perpendicular and horizontal angles. The telephone and telegraph systems were disrupted. And the great water-mains had burst. All the

---

[1] **nabobs**: rich and powerful people
[2] **lurid**: glowing through a haze

shrewd contrivances[1] and safeguards of man had been thrown out of gear by thirty seconds' twitching of the earth-crust.

Wednesday night saw the destruction of the very heart of the city. Dynamite was lavishly used, and many of San Francisco's proudest structures were crumbled by man himself into ruins, but there was no withstanding the onrush of the flames. Time and again successful stands were made by the fire-fighters, and every time the flames flanked around on either side or came up from the rear, and turned to defeat the hard-won victory.

Remarkable as it may seem, Wednesday night while the whole city crashed and roared into ruin, was a quiet night. There were no crowds. There was no shouting and yelling. There was no hysteria, no disorder. I passed Wednesday night in the path of the advancing flames, and in all those terrible hours I saw not one woman who wept, not one man who was excited, not one person who was in the slightest degree panic stricken.

Before the flames, throughout the night, fled tens of thousands of homeless ones. Some were wrapped in blankets. Others carried bundles of bedding and dear household treasures. Sometimes a whole family was harnessed to a carriage or delivery wagon that was weighted down with their possessions. Baby buggies, toy wagons, and go-carts were used as trucks, while every other person was dragging a trunk. Yet everybody was gracious. The most perfect **courtesy**[2] obtained. Never in all San Francisco's history, were her people so kind and courteous as on this night of terror.

---

[1] **shrewd contrivances**: clever inventions
[2] **courtesy**: good manners

A Caravan of Trunks

All night these tens of thousands fled before the flames. Many of them had fled all day as well. They had left their homes burdened with possessions. Now and again they lightened up, flinging out upon the street clothing and treasures they had dragged for miles.

They held on longest to their trunks, and over these trunks many a strong man broke his heart that night. The hills of San Francisco are steep, and up these hills, mile after mile, were the trunks dragged. Everywhere were trunks with across them lying their exhausted owners, men and women. Before the march of the flames were flung lines of soldiers. And a block at a time, as the flames advanced, these soldiers retreated. One of their tasks was to keep the trunk-pullers moving. The exhausted creatures, stirred on by the menace of **bayonets***, would arise and struggle up the steep pavements, pausing from weakness every five or ten feet.

Often, after surmounting a heart-breaking hill, they would find another wall of flame advancing upon them at right angles and be compelled to change anew the line of their retreat. In the end, completely played out, after toiling for a dozen hours like giants, thousands of them were compelled to abandon their trunks.

The Doomed City

At nine o'clock Wednesday evening I walked down through the very heart of the city. I walked through miles and miles of magnificent buildings and towering skyscrapers. Here was no fire. All was in perfect order. The police patrolled the streets. Every building had its watchman at the door. And yet it was doomed, all of it.

***bayonets**: knives on the ends of soldiers' guns

151

There was no water. The dynamite was giving out. And at right angles two different conflagrations were sweeping down upon it.

At one o'clock in the morning I walked down through the same section. Everything still stood intact. There was no fire. And yet there was a change. A rain of ashes was falling. The watchmen at the doors were gone. The police had been withdrawn. There were no firemen, no fire-engines, no men fighting with dynamite. The district had been absolutely abandoned. I stood at the corner of Kearny and Market, in the very innermost heart of San Francisco. Kearny Street was deserted. Half a dozen blocks away it was burning on both sides. The street was a wall of flame. And against this wall of flame, silhouetted sharply, were two United States **cavalrymen*** sitting their horses, calmly watching. That was all. Not another person was in sight. In the intact heart of the city two troopers sat their horses and watched.

A Fortune for a Horse!

It was at Union Square that I saw a man offering a thousand dollars for a team of horses. He was in charge of a truck piled high with trunks from some hotel. It had been hauled here into what was considered safety, and the horses had been taken out. The flames were on three sides of the Square and there were no horses.

An hour later, from a distance, I saw the truck-load of trunks burning merrily in the middle of the street.

On Thursday morning at a quarter past five, just twenty-four hours after the earthquake, I sat on the steps of a small residence on Nob Hill. To the east and south at right angles, were advancing two mighty walls of flame.

***cavalrymen**: soldiers on horseback

I went inside with the owner of the house on the steps of which I sat. He was cool and cheerful and hospitable. 'Yesterday morning,' he said, 'I was worth six hundred thousand dollars. This morning this house is all I have left. It will go in fifteen minutes.' He pointed to a large cabinet. 'That is my wife's collection of china. This rug upon which we stand is a present. It cost fifteen hundred dollars. Try that piano. Listen to its tone. There are few like it. There are no horses. The flames will be here in fifteen minutes.'

The Dawn of the Second Day

I passed out of the house. Day was trying to dawn through the smoke-pall. A sickly light was creeping over the face of things. Once only the sun broke through the smoke-pall, blood-red, and showing quarter its usual size. The smoke-pall itself, viewed from beneath, was a rose colour that pulsed and fluttered with lavender shades. Then it turned to mauve and yellow and dun. There was no sun. And so dawned the second day on **stricken*** San Francisco.

An hour later I was creeping past the shattered dome of the City Hall. Than it there was no better exhibit of the destructive force of the earthquake. Most of the stone had been shaken from the great dome, leaving standing the naked framework of steel. Market Street was piled high with the wreckage, and across the wreckage lay the overthrown pillars of the City Hall shattered into short crosswise sections.

Here and there through the smoke, creeping warily under the shadows of tottering walls, emerged occasional men and women. It was like the meeting of the handful of survivors after the day of the end of the world.

---

*stricken: suffering

Travellers' tales

The travellers whose tales are recounted here have many different reasons for making a journey. Some are leaving homes in Europe to start a new life in America, drawn by the prospect of better jobs or the hope of a more equal society. Some are seeking a personal challenge, using travel as a test of physical strength or mental endurance. And some are adventurous explorers drawn to remote regions of the world to learn about the local culture and discover both what is different about the peoples of the world and what we have in common.

The challenge for travel writers is to make their personal experiences interesting and relevant for readers who may never set foot in the countries they describe. To do this, some of the writers in this collection describe scenes and events in close detail, using words and images that appeal to our senses and help us imagine the scenes clearly. Others write in a more casual, conversational style, often using humour to reveal their personalities and their feelings about their experiences to the reader. As you read these travel accounts, think about what these writers have done to engage your interest. Look especially at why they have chosen to include particular details and at how they use language in interesting or striking ways to make scenes and events memorable.

Coming to New York at the turn of the Twentieth Century

Alistair Cooke

In the last hundred years, millions of people have gone to America in search of a better life – to find work or food, or to escape war and persecution. What was it like to make that kind of journey? Alistair Cooke, a British journalist who spent most of his working life in America and himself became an American citizen, tells the story of the immigrants who made modern America. In this extract he describes their arrival at New York and the beginning of a new life. Although the writer was not present at the events he describes, he creates a strong atmosphere in this piece. As you read:

- *think about the words he uses to create such vivid scenes and how he makes the reader feel sympathy towards the immigrants who came to New York.*

Long before they arrived at their **ports of embarkation*** – Constantinople, Piraeus, Antwerp, Bremen – emigrant trains had started deep inside Russia. Most of them were linked box cars, sometimes with benches, the men in one car, the women and children in another. Every few hundred miles the trains would be shunted on to a siding in order to pick up other new armies, of Austrians,

---

* **ports of embarkation**: ports of departure for America

Hungarians, Lithuanians, and finally a troop of Germans, before they came to, say, Hamburg. There they were **corralled**[1] and checked to see if they had the three essential passports to America; an exit paper, twenty-five spare dollars to prevent their becoming a public charge, and the price of the passage. By the 1890s lively rate wars between steamship lines had halved the fare from about twenty dollars to ten. In an enclosure outside Hamburg they would be bathed, de-loused, and fed, and their baggage and clothes fumigated. Then they were ferried out to the big ship and stowed aboard, as many as nine hundred in **steerage**[2].

In the floating commune of the emigrant ship, the status symbols were few but well defined. A suitcase, however battered, was most likely the mark of a city man. To a poor peasant, a wicker basket was elegance enough. Most people tied everything up in a blanket or a sheet. They had brought with them what they thought to be indispensable to a decent life afloat. First, the necessity of a pillow, goose-feather, if they were lucky – a point of pride, a relic, and a symbol that some families kept throughout their lives. Like all travellers, both simple and sophisticated, they were deeply suspicious of the other nation's food. It was a common thing to take along a cooking pot, a few raw vegetables, and a hunk of sausage or some other final reminder of the favourite snack. The religious took with

---

[1] **corralled**: herded together
[2] **steerage**: the cheapest accommodation on a ship

them the tokens of their faith, a cross or a prayer book; and a member of a close-knit family would cherish an heirloom. It could be nothing more pretentious than a brass candlestick or a lock of hair.

For two weeks or eight days, depending on the size of the ship, they sewed, played cards, sang to harmonicas or tin whistles, counted their savings, continually checked their exit papers, complained about the atrocious food and the rats. The ones who could read, probably less than half the flock, recited the cheering promise of the emigrants' agents' pamphlets. The young women nursed the elders and the chronically seasick and resisted, or succumbed to, the advances of **spry**[1] bachelors. There was no possibility of privacy in the swarm of steerage.

But as America came nearer, some of them suffered from nervous recall of the strategies that had got them this far. Bright youngsters who had carefully failed their high school examinations in order to prove their unfitness for military service. Oldsters who began to mask a fever with massive doses of medicine. Embezzlers, petty criminals, and **betrothed**[2] men skipping breach-of-promise suits who had obviously had the wit to fake an exit pass or steal the passage money. A lot of people had a lot to hide.

The harbour was sometimes choked with ships at anchor. In the early 1900s there could be as many as fifteen thousand immigrants arriving in one day, and the ships

---

[1] **spry**: lively
[2] **betrothed**: engaged

had to drop anchor and wait. But eventually the engines would rumble again, and there, like a battleship on the horizon, stood what the song calls 'Manhattan, an isle of joy'. Closer, it grew into a cluster of pinnacles known as skyscrapers. And then the mid-town skyscrapers topped the ones first seen. It was unlike any other city, and to the European it was always **audacious**[1] and magical, and threatening.

Soon the newcomers would be on the docks sorting their bundles and baggage in a babble of languages, and when that was done they were tagged with numbers then they were shipped aboard a ferry or a barge to what was to be known in several languages as 'the isle of tears', the clearing station, Ellis Island.

Today, it looks like a rather imposing college recently gutted by fire. It is totally derelict, a monument to the American habit of junking and forgetting whatever wears out. But wandering through its great central hall and tattered corridors, seeing the offices with their rusting files, the broken lavatories, and upturned dining tables, one can imagine the bedlam of its heyday, when the milling swarm of strangers was served and interrogated by hundreds of inspectors, wardens, interpreters, doctors, nurses, waiters, cooks, and agents of immigrant aid societies.

---

[1] **audacious**: daring

The newcomers crowded into the main building and the first thing they heard over the general **bedlam**[1] were the voices of inspectors bellowing out numbers in Italian, German, Polish, Hungarian, Russian and Yiddish. According to assigned numbers they were herded into groups of thirty and led through long tiled corridors up a wide staircase into the biggest hall most of them had ever seen. Its dimensions, its pillars, its great soaring windows still suggest the grand ballroom of some abdicated monarch. Once they were assembled there in their thousands, the clearance procedure began. I recently pressed an aged immigrant to describe it. 'Procedure?' he squealed incredulously. 'Din, confusion, bewilderment, madness!'

They moved in single file through a maze of passageways and under the eye of a doctor in a blue uniform who had in his hand a piece of chalk. He would look at the hands, the hair, the faces and rap out a few questions. He might spot a panting old man with purple lips, and he would chalk on his back a capital 'H' for suspected heart disease. Any facial blotches, a hint of gross eczema brought forth a chalked 'F', for facial rash. Children in arms were made to stand down to see if they rated an 'L' for limp rickets or some other deficiency disease. There was one chalk mark that every family dreaded, for it guaranteed certain deportation. It was a circle with a cross in the middle, and it indicated 'feeble-minded'.

---

[1] **bedlam**: chaos

Next they moved on to two doctors dipping into bowls of disinfectant and snapping back the eyelids of suspects, usually with a buttonhook. They were looking for a disease very common then in southern and eastern Europe, trachoma. If you had it, an 'E' was chalked on your back, and your first days in the New World were surely your last.

About eight in ten survived this scrutiny and passed to the final ordeal, the examination before an immigration inspector standing with an interpreter. Not noticeably gracious types, for they worked ten hours a day, seven days a week, they droned out an unchanging chant: Who paid your passage? How many dependents? Ever been in prison? Can you read and write? Is there a job waiting for you? (This was a famous catch, since a law called the Contract Labour Law forbade immigrants from signing up abroad for any work at all.) Finally, your name was checked against the ship's **manifest***. Many people were lucky to emerge into the new life with their old name. An Irish inspector glancing down at what to him was the gobbledygook of 'Oupenska' wrote on the landing card 'Spensky'. A Norwegian with an unpronounceable name was asked for the name of the town he had left. It was Dröbak. The inspector promptly wrote down what he thought he'd heard. Another Norwegian standing nearby philosophically realized that his own name was just as unmanageable and decided that what was good enough for his friend was good enough for him. To this day the

---

*manifest: list of passengers

children of both families rejoice in the name of Robeck.

But a new identity was better than none, and it gave you a landing card. With it you were now ready to pay a visit to a currency booth to change your lire or drachmas, or whatever, into dollars. At last you were handed over to the travel agent or the railroad men, if you were going far afield, or you sought the help of an aid society or a beckoning politician, if New York was to be the end of the line. Most immigrants could speak hardly a word of English except the one they had memorized as the town of their destination. A man would unfold a scrap of paper and point to a block-printed word: 'Pringvilliamas'. Maybe he eventually arrived in Springfield, Massachusetts, or maybe he didn't. But at this point the immigrants' only concern was to get off Ellis Island. All of them looked in relief for the door that was marked 'Push to New York'. And they pushed.

Now, after another ferry ride, they set foot in the land that was paved with gold. I once asked a successful but unfailingly cynical immigrant if the reality hadn't meant a shattering **disillusion***. 'But there *was* gold,' he said, 'to us. There were markets groaning with food and clothes. There were streetcars all over town. You could watch the automobiles. There was no military on horseback and no whips. The neighbours were out in the open, trading and shouting, enjoying free fights. And to a boy like me it was a ball, a friendship club. The streets were an open road.'

***disillusion**: disappointment

Going to New York

Frank McCourt

Some people travel to escape from troubles at home. The Irish writer Frank McCourt left Limerick in 1949 on a ship bound for New York. He was just 19 and was leaving behind the most appalling poverty and hardship. His father, who had already tried and failed to make his fortune in America in the 1930s, was an alcoholic who abandoned the family. His mother brought up the McCourt children on a diet of sugar water, bread and milk and watched three of them die from tuberculosis and pneumonia. In this last part of his autobiography, Angela's Ashes, *despite his excitement at starting a new life, McCourt has regrets about leaving his family. As you read:*

- *think about what is striking and unusual about this writer's style. Think about vocabulary choices, the way that sentences are varied and punctuated and how it sounds when you read it aloud.*

On my days off from work I walk around Limerick and look at all the places we lived, the Windmill Street, Hartstonge Street, Roden Lane, Rosbrien Road, Little Barrington Street, which is really a lane. I stand looking at Theresa Carmody's house till her mother comes out and says, What do you want? I sit at the graves of Oliver and Eugene in the old St. Patrick's Burying Ground and cross the road to St. Lawrence's Cemetery where Theresa is buried. Wherever I go I hear voices of the dead and I wonder if they can follow you across the Atlantic Ocean.

I want to get pictures of Limerick stuck in my head in case I never come back. I sit in St. Joseph's Church and the Redemptorist church and tell myself take a good look because I might never see this again. I walk down Henry Street to say good-bye to St. Francis though I'm sure I'll be able to talk to him in America.

Now there are days I don't want to go to America. I'd like to go to O'Riordan's Travel Agency and get back my fifty-five pounds. I could wait till I'm twenty-one and Malachy can go with me so that I'll know at least one person in New York. I have strange feelings and sometimes when I'm sitting by the fire with Mam and my brothers I feel tears coming and I'm ashamed of myself for being weak. At first Mam laughs and tells me, Your bladder must be near your eye, but then Michael says, We'll all go to America, Dad will be there, Malachy will be there and we'll all be together, and she gets the tears herself and we sit there, the four of us, like weeping **eejits**[1].

Mam says this is the first time we ever had a party and isn't it a sad thing altogether that you have it when your children are slipping away one by one, Malachy to England, Frank to America. She saves a few shillings from her wages taking care of Mr. Sliney to buy bread, ham, **brawn**[2], cheese, lemonade and a few bottles of stout. Uncle

---

[1] **eejits**: idiots (slang term)
[2] **brawn**: meat

Pa Keating brings stout, whiskey and a little sherry for Aunt Aggie's delicate stomach and she brings a cake loaded with currants and raisins she baked herself. The Abbot brings six bottles of stout and says, That's all right, Frankie, ye can all drink it as long as I have a bottle or two for meself to help me sing me song.

He sings "The Road to Rasheen." He holds his stout, closes his eyes, and song comes out in a high whine. The words make no sense and everyone wonders why tears are seeping from his shut eyes. Alphie whispers to me, Why is he crying over a song that makes no sense?

I don't know.

The Abbot ends his song, opens his eyes, wipes his cheeks and tells us that was a sad song about an Irish boy what went to America and got shot by gangsters and died before a priest could reach his side and he tells me don't be gettin' shot if you're not near a priest.

Uncle Pa says that's the saddest song he ever heard and is there any chance we could have something lively. He calls on Mam and she says, Ah, no, Pa, sure I don't have the wind.

Come on, Angela, come on. One voice now, one voice and one voice only.

All right. I'll try.

We all join in the chorus of her sad song,

> A mother's love is a blessing
> No matter where you roam.
> Keep her while you have her,
> You'll miss her when she's gone.

Uncle Pa says one song is worse than the one before and are we turning this night into a wake altogether, is there any chance someone would sing a song to liven up the proceedings or will he be driven to drink with the sadness.

Oh, God, says Aunt Maggie, I forgot. The moon is having an eclipse abroad this minute.

We stand out in the lane watching the moon disappear behind a round black shadow. Uncle Pa says, That's a very good sign for you going to America, Frankie.

No, says Aunt Aggie, 'tis a bad sign. I read in the paper that the moon is practicing for the end of the world.

Oh, end of the world my arse, says Uncle Pa. 'Tis the beginning for Frankie McCourt. He'll come back in a few years with a new suit and fat on his bones like any Yank and a lovely girl with white teeth hangin' from his arm.

Mam says, Ah, no, Pa, ah, no, and they take her inside and comfort her with a drop of sherry from Spain.

It's late in the day when the *Irish Oak* sails from Cork, past Kinsale and Cape Clear, and dark when lights twinkle on Mizen Head, the last of Ireland I'll see for God knows how long.

Surely I should have stayed, taken the post office examination, climbed in the world. I could have brought in enough money for Michael and Alphie to go to school with proper shoes and bellies well filled. We could have moved from the lane to a street or even an avenue where houses have gardens. I should have taken that examination and Mam would never again have to empty the chamber pots of Mr. Sliney or anyone else.

166

It's too late now. I'm on the ship and there goes Ireland into the night and it's foolish to be standing on this deck looking back and thinking of my family and Limerick and Malachy and my father in England and even more foolish that songs are going through my head Roddy McCorley goes to die and Mam gasping Oh the days of the Kerry dancing with poor Mr. Clohessy hacking away in the bed and now I want Ireland back at least I had Mam and my brothers and Aunt Aggie bad as she was and Uncle Pa, standing me my first pint, and my bladder is near my eye and here's a priest standing by me on the deck and you can see he's curious.

He's a Limerickman but he has an American accent from his years in Los Angeles. He knows how it is to leave Ireland, did it himself and never got over it. You live in Los Angeles with sun and palm trees day in day out and you ask God if there's any chance He could give you one soft rainy Limerick day.

The priest sits beside me at the table of the First Officer, who tells us ship's orders have been changed and instead of sailing to New York we're bound for Montreal.

Three days out and orders are changed again. We are going to New York after all.

Three American passengers complain, Goddam Irish. Can't they get it straight?

The day before we sail into New York orders are changed again. We are going to a place up the Hudson River called Albany.

The Americans say, Albany? Goddam Albany? Why

167

the hell did we have to sail on a goddam Irish tub? Goddam.

The priest tells me to pay no attention. All Americans are not like that.

I'm on the deck the dawn we sail into New York. I'm sure I'm in a film, that it will end and lights will come up in the Lyric Cinema. The priest wants to point out things but he doesn't have to. I can pick out the Statue of Liberty, Ellis Island, the Empire State Building, the Chrysler Building, the Brooklyn Bridge. There are thousands of cars speeding along the roads and the sun turns everything to gold. Rich Americans in top hats white ties and tails must be going home to bed with the gorgeous women with white teeth. The rest are going to work in warm comfortable offices and no one has a care in the world.

The pursuit of fear

Robert Macfarlane

Mountains have a powerful hold on our imagination. They can inspire fear, stun us with their beauty, or present the ultimate challenge of risking our lives to conquer their summits. Very few people who read Macfarlane's account will ever climb in the Alps, or face such extreme danger. Yet he paints a very vivid picture for us of his close brush with death and gives us an insight into what motivates him to risk his life "for a mountain". As you read:

- *think about the details the writer selects, and the techniques he uses, to make this account so dramatic and memorable.*

I looked upwards. A tall, steep face of rock, striped vertically with **snow gullies**[1], angled up into the lightening sky. That was our route. My eye followed the face down. Without relenting in angle, it dropped some 600 feet to a small **glacier**[2] which arced off the bottom of the face. The convex surface of the glacier looked hard, silvered and pitted like old metal, and it was pocked with stones which had fallen from the cliffs above. Further down, the glacier tumbled over a hundred-foot drop. There its surface turned a curdled grey, and the

---

[1] **snow gullies**: big snow-filled grooves in the side of a mountain
[2] **glacier**: a slow moving mass of ice

smoothness of the upper ice became ruptured into **crevasses**[1] and blocks. I could see glimmers of blue ice far down inside the body of the glacier. That was where we would end up if we fell.

We had left the hut too late that morning. When we stepped outside, the sky beyond the mountains to our east was already livid with colour. It meant the day would be a hot one; another good reason to have avoided a late start, for the warmth would loosen rocks that were gripped by ice, and cause crevasses to yawn in the glaciers. Pushing for time and unroped, we half-jogged up over two steepening miles of glacier, trusting the lingering cold to keep the snow-bridges rigid. A final toil up a long snow ramp – tacking back and forth to make the slope less severe – brought us to the shoulder of our mountain, and the beginning of the route.

The main problem was scree, the debris of small stones and rock chips which collects on mountainsides. Scree is despised by mountaineers for two reasons. First, because it can easily be pushed off on to you by people climbing above. And second, because it makes every step you take insecure. Put a foot down on a shoal of scree, and it'll skid off as the scree scrapes over the rock beneath.

For about thirty minutes we moved steadily up the rock face. The rock was in poor condition, shattered horizontally and mazed with cracks. When I tried to haul

---

[1] **crevasses**: big cracks in the ice

170

myself up on a block of it, it would pull out towards me, like a drawer opening. Some of the rock ledges were covered with a moist sill of snow. My hands became progressively wetter and colder. The climbing hardware we had **festooned*** about us clanked and tinkled on the rock. This, our breathing and the rasp of rock on rock were the only noises.

Then came a shout. *'Cailloux! Cailloux!'* I heard yelled from above, in a female voice. The words echoed down towards us. I looked up to see where they had come from.

Time doesn't stop or slow down when you are in danger. Everything happens as fast. It's just that – providing we survive them – we subject these periods of time to such intense retrospective scrutiny that we come to know them more fully, more exactly. We see them in freeze-frame. From this moment I remember a rivulet of water running darkly down the rock-rib in front of my eyes, the minute cross-hatchings on the fabric of my waterproof jacket and a little yellow Alpine flower tucked into a pocket of rock. And a sound – the crunching of the scree beneath my feet as I braced myself for the impact.

There were just two rocks at first, leaping and bounding down the face towards us, once cannoning off each other in mid-air. And then the air above suddenly seemed alive with falling rocks, humming through the air and filling it with noise. *Crack*, went each one as it leapt off the rock face, then *hum-hum-hum* as it moved through the air, then

---

***festooned**: draped

171

crack again. The pause between the cracks lengthened each time, as the rocks gained momentum and jumped further and further.

Up above us, two French climbers glanced beneath their legs. They watched as the single rock which they had nudged off a ledge dislodged several other rocks, and those some others, and suddenly a gang of rocks of different sizes was leaping noisily off down the face. They couldn't see properly whether there was anyone below them: a protruding hood of rock prevented them getting a full view of the face. But it seemed unlikely that anyone would be coming up beneath them. They were the first down the mountain, having been turned back by a difficult pitch at the top. There had been no one coming across the glacier from where they had reached their high point. And no one would have been stupid enough to come later than that. But they shouted anyway, out of decorum; like calling 'fore' on an empty golf course.

I continued to gaze up at the rocks as they fell and skipped towards me. A boy who had been a few years above me at school had taught me never to look up during a rockfall. 'Why? Because a rock in your face is far less pleasant than a rock on your helmet,' he told us. 'Face in, always face in.' He had led us all day on a horseshoe walk in Wales, and then when we returned, exhausted, to the car park and the minibus, he had marched back off into the hills in the sludgy dusk light with a rope over his shoulder, to climb until he could no longer see. A year later he and a friend were killed by rockfall in the Alps.

172

I heard Toby, my partner on the mountain that day, shouting at me. I looked across. He was safe beneath an overhanging canopy of rock. I couldn't understand what he was saying. Then I felt a thump, and was tugged backwards and round, as though somebody had clamped a heavy hand on my shoulder and turned me to face them. No pain, but the blow had almost jerked me off my stance. The rock, which had hit the lid of my rucksack, bounced off towards the blue crevasses far below.

Rocks were spinning past now, maybe a dozen of them. I looked up again. A rock was heading down straight towards me. Instinctively, I leant backwards and arched my back out from the rock to try to protect my chest. What about my fingers, though, I thought; they'll be crushed flat if it hits them, and I'll never get down. Then I heard a *crack* directly in front of me, and a tug at my trousers, and a yell from Toby.

'Are you all right? That went straight through you.'

The rock had pitched in front of me, and passed through the hoop of my body, between my legs, missing me but snatching at my clothing as it went.

I looked up again, and watched as the last, and biggest, of the boulders fell towards me. I was directly in its line again. About forty feet above me it took a big hop off a rock, and spun out into the air. As I watched it come it grew larger, and darker, until it was the size of my head. With a sharp report it struck the rock face once more, then took a lateral leap to my left, and whirred away past me.

173

I realized I was gripping the rock in front of me so hard that my fingers were white at their tips. My limbs were shivering and seemed barely able to support my weight. My heart **pistoned***. But it was over. I promised myself yet again that I would never come back to the high mountains. 'Let's get off this hill,' I shouted across to Toby.

Trekking cautiously back across the glacier, unnerved, my body still trembling from the adrenaline, testing the soft snow for crevasses, we heard the characteristic *whop-whop-whop* of a helicopter give the valley a rhythm. I began to sing aloud the chopper song from *Full Metal Jacket*: 'Surfin' Bird' – the Trashmen cover. Then I stopped. Get a grip, I told myself. You're not in Vietnam, you're in the Alps, just a guy who's gone up into the mountains to scare himself, and succeeded. The helicopter's not for you.

It wasn't, either. It beat a path of sound over the glacier and thumped its way off east, towards the pinnacle of the Zinalrothorn, where somebody else had died.

Late that night, back in the valley and unable to sleep, I got out of our tent and walked about the campsite, stepping carefully over the guy-ropes. Torches were on inside some of the other tents and they looked like little orange igloos against the blackness of the cold meadow. The sky was clear, and the tilted snowfields on the upper slopes of the mountains flashed the moonlight down the valley like signalling mirrors.

***pistoned**: jumped

174

As I walked, I thought back over the day. Toby and I had spent the evening in a bar, drinking pints of lager in celebration of our near-miss. The room was full of smoke and other climbers, clunking from table to bar and back again in heavy plastic boots, shouting out their tales over the music. We had sat and talked through the events of the morning: what if the big final stone hadn't leapt sideways, what if I'd been knocked off, would you have held me, would I have pulled you off? A more experienced mountaineer would probably have thought nothing of it, filed it away in the bulging folder of near-misses, and carried on regardless. I knew I would not forget it. We had talked, too, about how much pleasure the fear had brought afterwards. And we had talked, as mountaineers always do, about how strange it is to risk yourself for a mountain, but how central to the experience is that risk and the fear it brings with it.

A Walk in the Woods

Bill Bryson

The Appalachian Trail in America stretches for over 2000 miles from Georgia to Maine across a landscape of mountains, forests and lakes – a vast area of wilderness in the most developed country in the world. In this extract from A Walk in the Woods, *Bill Bryson describes part of his journey along the trail with his friend Katz. Much of the trip is uneventful yet the reader is kept interested and entertained throughout. As you read:*

- *think about the techniques used by the writer to make ordinary events amusing and memorable.*

We fell into a simple routine. Each morning we rose at first light, shivering and rubbing arms, made coffee, broke camp, ate a couple of fistfuls of raisins, and set off into the silent woods. We would walk from about half past seven to four. We seldom walked together – our paces didn't match – but every couple of hours I would sit on a log (always surveying the surrounding undergrowth for the rustle of bear or boar) and wait for Katz to catch up, to make sure everything was OK. The trail was much harder for him than for me, and to his credit he tried not to bitch. It never escaped me for a moment that he didn't have to be there.

I had thought we would have a jump on the crowds, but there was a fair scattering of other hikers, perhaps two dozen of us altogether in the same general neck of the woods, all heading north. Because everyone walks at different rates and rests at different times, three or four times a day you bump into some or all of your fellow hikers, especially on mountaintops with panoramic views or beside streams with good water, and above all at the wooden shelters that stand at distant intervals, **ostensibly**[1] but not always actually, a day's hike apart in clearings just off the trail. In consequence you get to know your fellow hikers at least a little, quite well if you meet them nightly at the shelters. You become part of an informal clump, a loose and sympathetic **affiliation**[2] of people from different age groups and walks of life but all experiencing the same weather, same discomforts, same landscapes, same eccentric impulse to hike to Maine.

Even at busy times, however, the woods are great providers of solitude, and I encountered long periods of perfect aloneness, when I didn't see another soul for hours, and many times when I would wait for Katz for a long spell and no other hiker would come along. When that happened, I would leave my pack and go back and find him, to see that he was all right, which always pleased him. Sometimes he would be proudly bearing my stick, which I had left by a tree when I stopped to tie my laces or adjust my pack. We seemed to be looking out for each other. It was very nice. I can put it no other way.

---

[1] **ostensibly**: supposedly
[2] **affiliation**: group or club

Around four we would find a spot to camp, and pitch our tents. One of us would go off to fetch and filter water while the other prepared a sludge of steamy noodles. Sometimes we would talk, but mostly we existed in a kind of companionable silence. By six o'clock, dark and cold and weariness would force us to our tents. Katz went to sleep instantly, as far as I could tell. I would read for an hour or so then I would put myself in darkness and lie there listening to the peculiarly clear, articulated noises of the forest at night, the sighs and fidgets of wind and leaves, the weary groan of boughs, the endless murmurings and stirrings, like the noises of a **convalescent ward**[1] after lights out, until at last I fell heavily asleep. In the morning we would rise shivering and rubbing arms, wordlessly repeat our small chores, fill and hoist our packs and venture into the great entangling forest again.

On the fourth evening we made a friend. We were sitting in a nice little clearing beside the trail, our tents pitched, eating our noodles, savouring the exquisite pleasure of just sitting, when a plumpish, bespectacled young woman in a red jacket and the customary outsized pack came along. She regarded us with the crinkled squint of someone who is either chronically confused or can't see very well. We exchanged hellos and the usual **banalities**[2] about the weather and where we were. Then she squinted at the gathering gloom and announced she would camp with us.

---

[1] **convalescent ward**: a place where people recover from illness

[2] **banalities**: boring remarks

Her name was Mary Ellen. She was from Florida, and she was, as Katz for ever after termed her in a special tone of awe, a piece of work. She talked non-stop, except when she was clearing out her **Eustachian tubes***, which she did frequently, by pinching her nose and blowing out with a series of violent and alarming snorts of a sort that would make a dog leave the sofa and get under a table in the next room. I have long known that it is part of God's plan for me to spend a little time with each of the most stupid people on earth, and Mary Ellen was proof that even in the Appalachian woods I would not be spared. It became evident from the first moment that she was a rarity.

'So what are you guys eating?' she said, plonking herself down on a spare log and lifting her head to peer into our bowls. 'Noodles? Big mistake. Noodles have got like no energy. I mean like zero.' She unblocked her ears. 'Is that a Starship tent?'

I looked at my tent. 'I don't know.'

'Big mistake. They must have seen you coming at the camping store. What did you pay for it?'

'I don't know.'

'Too much, that's how much. You should have got a three-season tent.'

'It is a three-season tent.'

'Pardon me saying so, but it is like seriously dumb to come out here in March without a three-season tent.' She unblocked her ears.

---

*Eustachian tubes: the tube between the nose and the ear

179

'It is a three-season tent.'

'You're lucky you haven't froze yet. You should go back and like punch out the guy that sold it to you because he's been like, you know, negligible selling you that.'

'Believe me, it is a three-season tent.'

She unblocked her ears and shook her head impatiently. 'That's a three-season tent.'

She indicated Katz's tent.

'*That*'s exactly the same tent.'

She glanced at it again. 'Whatever. How many miles did you do today?'

'About ten.' Actually we had done eight point four – but this had included several formidable **escarpments**[1], including a notable wall of hell called Preaching Rock, the highest **eminence**[2] since Springer Mountain, for which we had awarded ourselves bonus miles, for purposes of morale.

'Ten miles? Is that all? You guys must be like *really* out of shape. I did fourteen-two.'

'How many have your lips done?' said Katz, looking up from his noodles.

She fixed him with one of her more severe squints. 'Same as the rest of me, of course.' She gave me a private look as if to say, 'Is your friend like seriously *weird* or something?' She cleared her ears. 'I started at Gooch Gap.'

'So did we. That's only eight point four miles.'

---

[1] **escarpments**: steep slopes
[2] **eminence**: hill

She shook her head sharply, as if shooing a particularly tenacious fly. 'Fourteen-two.'

'No, really, it's only eight point four.'

'Excuse me, but I just *walked* it. I think I ought to know.' And then suddenly: 'God, are those Timberland boots? *Mega* mistake. How much did you pay for them?'

And so it went. Eventually I went off to swill out the bowls and hang the food bag. When I came back, she was fixing her own dinner, but still talking away at Katz.

'You know what your problem is?' she was saying. 'Pardon my French, but you're too fat.'

Katz looked at her in quiet wonder. 'Excuse me?'

'You're too fat. You should have lost weight before you came out here. Shoulda done some training, 'cause you could have like a serious, you know, heart thing out here.'

'Heart thing?'

'You know, when your heart stops and you like, you know, die.'

'Do you mean a heart attack?'

'That's it.'

Mary Ellen, it should be noted, was not short on flesh herself, and unwisely at that moment she leaned over to get something from her pack, displaying an expanse of backside on which you could have projected motion pictures for, let us say, an army base. It was an interesting test of Katz's **forbearance***. He said nothing, but rose to go for a pee and out of the side of his mouth as he passed me

---

*forbearance: patience and willingness to forgive

181

he rendered a certain convenient expletive as three low, dismayed syllables, like the call of a freight train in the night.

The next day, as always, we rose chilled and feeling wretched, and set about the business of attending to our small tasks, but this time with the additional strain of having our every move examined and rated. While we ate raisins and drank coffee with flecks of toilet paper in it, Mary Ellen gorged on a multi-course breakfast of oatmeal, Pop Tarts, trail mix and a dozen small squares of chocolate, which she lined up in a row on the log beside her. We watched like orphaned refugees while she plumped her **jowls*** with food and enlightened us as to our shortcomings with regard to diet, equipment and general manliness.

And then, now a trio, we set off into the woods. Mary Ellen walked sometimes with me and sometimes with Katz, but always with one of us. It was apparent that for all her bluster she was majestically inexperienced and untrailworthy – she hadn't the faintest idea how to read a map, for one thing – and ill at ease on her own in the wilderness. I couldn't help feeling a little sorry for her. Besides, I began to find her strangely entertaining. She had the most extraordinarily redundant turn of phrase. She would say things like 'There's a stream of water over there', and 'It's nearly ten o'clock a.m.'. Once, in reference to winters in central Florida, she solemnly informed me,

---

*__jowls__: cheeks

182

'We usually get frosts once or twice a winter, but this year we had 'em a couple of times.' Katz for his part clearly dreaded her company and winced beneath her tireless urgings to smarten his pace.

We laboured four miles up and over Blood Mountain, at 4,461 feet the highest and toughest eminence on the trail in Georgia, then began a steep and exciting two-mile descent towards Neels Gap. Exciting because there was a shop at Neels Gap, at a place called the Walasi-Yi Inn, where you could buy sandwiches and ice cream. At about half past one, we heard a novel sound – motor traffic – and a few minutes later we emerged from the woods onto US Highway 19 and 129, which despite having two numbers was really just a back road through a high pass between wooded nowheres. Directly across the road was the Walasi-Yi Inn, a combination of hiking outfitters, grocery, bookshop and youth hostel. We hastened across the road – positively scurried across – and went inside.

Now it may seem to stretch credibility to suggest that things like a paved highway, the whoosh of passing cars and a proper building could seem exciting and unfamiliar after five days in the woods, but in fact it was so. Just passing through a door, being inside, surrounded by walls and a ceiling, was **novel***. And the Walasi-Yi's stuff was – well, I can't begin to describe how wonderful it was. There was a single modest-sized chilled cabinet filled with fresh sandwiches, soft drinks, cartons of juice and perishables

---

***novel**: unusual and exciting

like cheese, and Katz and I stared into it for ages, dumbly captivated. I was beginning to learn that the central feature of life on the Appalachian Trail is deprivation, that the whole point of the experience is to remove yourself so thoroughly from the conveniences of everyday life that the most ordinary things – processed cheese, a can of pop gorgeously beaded with condensation – fill you with wonder and gratitude. It is an intoxicating experience to taste Coca-Cola as if for the first time and to be conveyed to the very brink of orgasm by white bread. Makes all the discomfort worthwhile.

Katz and I bought two egg salad sandwiches each, some crisps, chocolate bars and soft drinks, and went with them to a picnic table outside, where we ate with greedy smackings and expressions of rapture, then returned to the chill cabinet to stare in wonder some more. The Walasi-Yi, we discovered, provided other services to bona fide hikers for a small fee – laundry centre, showers, towel hire – and we greedily availed ourselves of all those. The shower was a dribbly, antiquated affair, but the water was hot and I have never, and I mean never, enjoyed a grooming experience more. I watched with the profoundest satisfaction as five days of grime ran down my legs and into the drainhole, and noticed with astonished gratitude that my body had taken on a noticeably **svelter*** profile. We did two loads of laundry, washed out our cups and food bowls and pots and pans, bought and sent postcards,

***svelter**: slimmer

phoned home, and stocked up liberally on fresh and packaged foods in the shop.

We packed our purchases on the porch and realized together in the same instant, with joy and amazement, that Mary Ellen was no longer part of our retinue. I put my head in the door and asked if they had seen her.

'Oh, I think she left about an hour ago.'

Things were getting better and better.

It was after four o'clock by the time we set off again. There was a natural meadow ideal for camping about an hour's walk further on. The trail was warmly inviting in late afternoon sunlight – there were long shadows from the trees and expansive views across a river valley to stout, charcoal-coloured mountains – and the meadow was indeed a perfect place to camp. We pitched our tents and ate sandwiches, crisps and soft drinks we had bought for dinner.

Then, with as much pride as if I had baked them myself, I brought out a little surprise – two packets of Hostess cupcakes.

Katz's face lit up like a birthday boy.

'Oh, wow!'

'They didn't have any **Little Debbies***,' I apologized.

'Hey,' he said, 'hey.' He was lost for greater eloquence. Katz loved cakes.

We ate three of the cupcakes between us, and left the last one on the log, where we could admire it, for later. We

---

***Little Debbies**: an American brand of cake

were lying there, propped against logs, burping, smoking, feeling rested and content, talking for once — in short, acting much as I had envisioned it in my more optimistic moments back home – when Katz let out a low groan. I followed his gaze to find Mary Ellen striding briskly down the trail towards us from the wrong direction.

'I *wondered* where you guys had got to,' she scolded. 'You know, you are like *really* slow. We could've done another four miles by now easy. I can see I'm going to have to keep my eyes on you from now – Say, is that a Hostess cupcake?' Before I could speak or Katz could seize a log with which to **smite*** her dead, she said, 'Well, I don't mind if I do,' and ate it in two bites.

It would be some days before Katz smiled again.

**smite*: strike

Into the Heart of Borneo

Redmond O'Hanlon

Travel can be mentally and physically challenging. How well do you think you would cope if you had to hunt for your own food or share a jungle campsite with an army of inch-long, biting ants? Could you keep a sense of humour? The naturalist Redmond O'Hanlon found out the answers to these questions when he journeyed into the tropical jungle of Borneo with his friend, James Fenton, a poet. The SAS gave them advice and equipment and local guides led them on a long river voyage in wooden canoes. Here, they set up camp for the night. As you read:

- *think about the techniques used by the writer that make his account humorous and entertaining.*

Our beds had been expertly set up: two poles run through the specially designed tubes of the SAS **tarpaulins**[1] to form a stretcher, itself supported on a rectangular frame, a four-poster, lashed together with **rattan**[2] strips and awaiting only a mosquito net and a cover. Tying the net and the canvas roof to the surrounding trees with parachute cord, a small bed-length of insect-free security emerged in the jungle. Campaign-proved, everything fitted, tied together, over-lapped, held fast.

---

[1] **tarpaulins**: waterproof canvasses
[2] **rattan**: a type of plant, used to make wicker

187

Dana and Leon had almost finished building their own shelter. Having constructed a platform of poles about two feet off the jungle floor, they were laying a lattice-work of branches to make a sloping roof. Inghai returned from the hillside with bundles of enormous palm leaves, and the structure was complete. Lying inside on a leaf-bed, one's feet towards the four-foot opening overlooking the river, the roof coming down at a bright green angle tight above one's head, it seemed the childhood tree-house *par excellence*.

Dana then began to build his own little house. Six-foot tall, two-feet square, with a conventional triangular roof and a small platform halfway up, its use was not apparent. For the spirits?

'For fish,' said Leon, 'for smoking fish. Now we show you how to fish like the Iban.'

Taking their wooden harpoons from the canoe, Leon and Inghai dived into the river; and disappeared completely, like a pair of Great crested grebe. A full forty seconds later they bobbed up again, right over on the far bank. Leon stood up and held an enormous fish above his head, harpooned through the flank. Inghai, as befitted his size, held up a tiddler. Much yelling in Iban took place. Dana, evidently stung into action, took a large weighted net out of the canoe, a jala, and made his way upstream to the shingle bank. Swinging it back and forth in both hands, swaying slightly, he cast it out; a slowly spinning circle of white mesh settled on the water, and sank. Jumping in, scrabbling about to collect the bottom ends of the net, Dana finally scooped it all up again, together with three catfish. They looked at us **lugubriously***, an immensely long whisker or barbel, their feelers drooping down from either side of their mouths. Dana detached them with greatest care, avoiding their dorsal and pectoral spines which, presumably, were poisonous, and tossed them up the shingle.

Leon and Inghai returned with six fish, all of the same species, *Sebarau*, handsome, streamlined, and, unlike the smooth and mucus-covered catfish, armoured with large silver scales and adorned with a bold black bar down each side.

Inghai collected driftwood and made two fires, one on the beach and the other at the base of the smoking-house. Leon gutted the fish, cut them into sections, placed some in a salt tin, some on the smoking-rack, and some in a water-filled cooking pot. Two ancient cauldrons, slung from a high wooden frame, bubbling over the fire: one full of fish pieces and one full of sticky rice. Dana, having set a larger net part-across the current, supported by ropes to an overhanging branch and by white polystyrene floats, returned for supper.

Dusk came suddenly, and, equally suddenly, Eared nightjars appeared, hawking insects, stooping and turning in their haphazard bat-like way, along the tops of the trees above the river banks, seeming half-transparent and weightless in their ghostly agility, like falcons weirdly deprived of their power and strike and push. And they were whistling to each other.

*****lugubriously**: sadly and gloomily

After ten minutes, they vanished. Which was just as well, because it had dawned on me that the fish and rice in my mess-tin would need all the attention I could give it. The sebarau was tasteless, which did not matter, and full of bones, which did. It was like a hair-brush caked in lard. James had made the same discovery.

'Redmond, don't worry,' he whispered, 'if you need a **tracheotomy*** I have a biro-tube in my baggage.'

It was time to go to bed. We washed our mess-tins in the river, kicked out the fire on the beach, and stoked up the smoking-house fire with more wet logs. Slinging my soaking clothes from a tree with parachute cord, I rubbed myself down with a wet towel and, naked, opened my Bergen to pull out my set of dry kit for the night. Every nook and cranny in the bag was alive with inch-long ants. Deciding that anything so huge must be the Elephant ant, and not the Fire ant, which packs a sting like a wasp, I brushed the first wave off my y-fronts. Glancing up, I was astonished to see my wet clothes swarming with ants, too; a procession of dark ants poured down one side of the rope and up the other, and, all over my wet trousers, hundreds of different moths were feeding. Darkness seemed to rise from the leafy mush of the forest floor; and I rummaged quickly in the outside Bergen pocket for my army torch. As my fingers closed on it, everyone else's little fingers seemed to close on my arm. I drew it out fast

---

***tracheotomy**: an operation performed by cutting a hole in someone's throat when their windpipe has been blocked

and switched on: Elephant ants, this time with massive pincers, were suspended from hand to elbow. The soldiers had arrived. I flicked them off, gratified to hear yelps from James's basha as I did so. It was good to know they also went for poets.

Slipping under the mosquito net, I fastened myself into the dark-green camouflage SAS tube. It seemed luxuriously comfortable. You had to sleep straight out like a rifle; but the ants, swarming along the poles, rearing up on their back legs to look for an entry, and the mosquitoes, whining and singing outside the various tunes of their species in black shifting clouds, could not get in.

'Eeeeeee – ai – yack yack yack yack yack!' Something screamed in my ear, with brain-shredding force. And then everyone joined in.

'Eeeeeee – ai – yack yack yack yack yack te yooo!' answered every other giant male cicada, maniacally vibrating the tymbals, drumskin membranes in their cavity amplifiers, the megaphones built into their bodies.

'Shut up!' I shouted.

'Wah Wah Wah Wah Wah!' said four thousand frogs.

'Stop it at once!' yelled James.

'Clatter clitter clatter' went our mess-tins over the shingle, being nosed clean by tree shrews.

The Iban laughed. The river grew louder in the darkness. Something screamed in earnest further off. Something shuffled and snuffled around the discarded rice and fish bits flung in a bush from our plates. A porcupine? A civet? A ground squirrel? The long-tailed giant rat? Why not a clouded leopard? Or, the only really dangerous mammal in Borneo, the long-clawed, short-tempered Sun bear?

I switched off the torch and tried to sleep. But it was no good. The decibel-level was way over the limit allowed in discotheques. And, besides, the fire-flies kept flicking their own torches on and off; and some kind of phosphorescent fungus glowed in the dark like a forty-watt bulb.

I switched on again, clipped the right-angled torch on to my shirt, and settled down for a peaceful bedtime read.

Makalla

Freya Stark

Nowadays, package tours and cheap air fares make it easy to travel to exotic destinations which were once closed to foreigners. Freya Stark, a remarkable woman who died in 1993 aged 100, wrote more than thirty books about her intrepid travels in the first half of the twentieth century. She travelled alone to remote regions, such as the Arabian Peninsula, where she mixed with Sultans and Bedouin tribespeople, mapped the region for the first time, discovered lost cities and even established an anti-Nazi spy ring. However, even in these remote places, the way of life that Freya Stark described was changing. Here, she visits schools in the Yemen, which at that time was governed by Britain. As you read:

- *think about the writer's eye for detail as she describes aspects of her visit. What surprises or interests her about the schools in Makalla?*

I visited three schools in Makalla before I left. The new and handsome one, only five years old, is paid for by the Sultan and provides six years of education free to all who want it; but the teachers told me that they can rarely persuade a boy's parents to leave him for more than four years, for there is no material advantage in education.

The teachers were young and eager, with that love of learning for its own sake of which the East is not yet ashamed. There were thirteen of them, to about 300 boys in six classes. The two smallest classes sat cross-legged on the floor; the older ones had benches, and all – from the tiniest – could produce a welcoming poem, uttered with appropriate gestures and more or less **acute**[1] signs of misery, but with obvious feeling for social obligation behind it. The children were ragged, and unintelligent to look at, as is the way of insanitary towns: and books, that come from Egypt, were few. The great treasure was a globe on a stand, kept in a bag for great occasions; two big maps, a few readers, and many Qurans provided the pasture; and five of the subjects taught were various aspects of the Quran: the rest were reading, grammar, dictation, composition, drawing, arithmetic, geometry, geography, history, and signalling with flags – the culminating point of education, and kept for the last and most advanced class as a climax to be looked forward to across the **arid**[2] spaces of five preliminary years. Sayyid 'Omar, the assistant head, who took me round, was kind and gentle and fond of his children: he had the long face, little chin beard, almond-shaped eyes and large and well-cut mouth which is typical in **Hadhramaut**[3] – an aristocratic type Van Dyck might have painted: and his enthusiasm and that of Shaikh 'Abdullah, who kept the school register, gave a pleasant feeling to the place in spite of the poverty of the scholars and the gigantic task undertaken with means so inadequately slender.

---

[1] **acute**: severe

[2] **arid**: dry

[3] **Hadhramaut**: the area around Makalla

The old government school was on the same lines, but the third was a private venture conducted by an Indian Christian missionary, who had fifty-five pupils, much cleaner and better dressed than Sayyid 'Omar's flock, but all more or less fatally affected by the disease of smugness which oriental Christians often seem to take over inadvertently from the **Pharisees***. No one had wanted the Missionary in Makalla, which prides itself on admitting no Jews and hardly any Christians, and he had to wait many months before being allowed to settle there at all; and now here he was with kind conscientious face and yellow teeth and spectacles, getting sixty rupees a month from the Sultan to run his school, provide his scholars with stationery and all they might require, and keep himself and his family alive. In his lodging upstairs he had two rows of books well thumbed to guide him on his way, a thin little wife who tried to make the best of things, and small girls whose mission lessons in embroidery were, said the wife, being forgotten. I saw the embroidery, and did not think this an unmixed evil; some things are better forgotten. But I admired the heroism that fed the struggling spirit, wrestling alone to impart an unassimilated civilization in an unwilling land. The assembled classes sang me "God Save the King", in English and then in Arabic: I listened with some misgiving, wondering if this might not be misinterpreted as one of these subtle British arts of propaganda which we are always

---

* **Pharisees**: an ancient Jewish group known for their strict interpretation of religious law

hearing about – but I afterwards learned that "God Save the King" is an accomplishment of which all Makalla is proud, and has no territorial implications.

The most amusing performance in the school was an English dialogue between two of the younger scholars, about a chair.

'I have bought a chair,' said one.

'What is it like?' asked the other.

'It is made of wood,' ... etc. etc.

It sounds a peaceful and amicable conversation. But the two lads pitched into it as if it were a battle, at the top of their voices and with incredible fury, leaning towards each other as if the physical interposition of thirty-odd fellow scholars alone kept them from each other's throats. It was only by listening carefully that I felt reassured as to its being merely the description of a chair.

The polo match

Michael Palin

In 2004 Michael Palin spent six months travelling in the Himalaya with a BBC camera crew. In the Pakistani village of Chitral, he attended their annual polo match against nearby Gilgit, a spectacular event which took place high in the mountains at the Shandur Pass. Here he describes the festivities and the mounting tension in the build up to the game, as well as the spectacle and excitement of the big match. Palin is interested in discovering the customs and traditions of a culture that is very different from his own, but also in recognising what is familiar. As you read:

- *think about how he describes unusual sights and events in a way that we can all understand and relate to.*

Day Sixteen

There are three big polo games over the next three days. The two villages nearest the pass, Laspur on the Chitral side and Ghiza on the Gilgit side, play each other today. Tomorrow is the turn of the Chitral and Gilgit 'B' teams, and the final day is the big match between the 'A' sides.

The Laspur team is camped, modestly, a mile or so back towards the pass. With only an hour to go before the game, supporters are still arriving, many of them walking up the long steep road from the village. Before they leave for the ground each player seeks the blessing of the elders of the village. Meanwhile, their supporters sit around listening to music. Various men (there are no women to be seen) are moved to dance. One of them moves particularly gracefully. My guide whispers in my ear.

'He is Taliban.'

During a break in the dancing there is an address from a man in a dirty *shalwar-kameez*[1], with a stick, a pack and leathery, sun-scorched features. Whether he intends to look like the classic **yokel**[2] or not I don't know, but it's clear from the way the audience listens that he is a star, and a comedy star at that. My guide tries to translate but the laughs come so thick and fast that he has trouble keeping up.

It's all good anti-government stuff. According to my guide, it's a popular **grouse**[3] on both sides of the Pass that the government praises the spirit of the mountain communities but fails to put any money their way.

Like any good comedian his eyes flick round the audience, and pretty soon alight on me. To gales of laughter he tells me that his people pray constantly for the restoration of British rule and he asks me to tell the Queen that if she gives them each a thousand rupees she can have their village back.

Meanwhile, the players are emerging from a team talk and are getting ready to mount their horses. In their red jerseys, white *pakol* hats, red knee pads and black boots

---

[1] *shalwar-kameez*: long tunic and baggy trousers
[2] **yokel**: country bumpkin
[3] **grouse**: complaint

they stand out like mediaeval knights among the rough and ready dress of the villagers. The captain, a wiry middle-aged man wearing dark glasses, caresses his horse's head and talks soothingly into its ear.

A fiercely fought game sees Laspur coming in to win an 8-7 victory. The crowd pour onto the pitch and no-one tries to stop them. The quiet, rather studious figure I saw whispering soothing confidences to his horse two hours ago is the hero of the day, flung up onto the shoulders of rapturous supporters. First blood to the Chitral Valley. Hopefully, it will be a good omen.

Day Seventeen

More people have arrived overnight and our encampment is now part of a growing community. Figures are scattered among the grassy boulders, cleaning teeth, scrubbing feet and washing faces in bowls of water heated on a brushwood fire, which Maboub, who is in charge of these matters, has to keep continually tended, as thinner air at this height make things harder to burn. In the kitchen tent, where a violent gas fire looks like an accident waiting to happen, Zahoor, the chef, produces scrambled eggs, fried potatoes and even porridge for our breakfast.

At the far end of the valley, away from the hustle and bustle of the ever-expanding encampment, the 'A' teams are out beside the lake practising shots, gallops, passes and tight-reined turns. Both sides exercise together in the cool of early morning, then return to their separate camps.

Gilgit's team is drawn entirely from the ranks of police and army. They're well-drilled, organized, efficient but institutional. Their captain, Bulbul Jan, is a tall middle-aged man with neat, short hair and the modest, kindly manner of an **avuncular**[1] schoolmaster. Hard to believe as he talks softly to us that he is one half of the most successful combination in free-style polo. The other is his tall, black Punjabi stallion, Truc.

Bulbul is 55 and his horse is 21. Together they have played in 15 of these matches and have led Gilgit to victory for the last two years, proving that despite the Herculean efforts required of them up here on the plateau, **guile**[2] and experience still count as much as youth and strength. Bulbul claims that Truc can tell him, within 24 hours of a game, just how things will work out.

'So what about your chances tomorrow?'

Truc bares his teeth and rears his head away, clearly impatient to end the interview.

'Truc is in a very good mood,' pronounces Bulbul Jan.

Chitral come across as the gentlemen amateurs, with an altogether more happy-go-lucky approach to their polo, but the mood at the camp today is subdued. Gilgit won the 'B' game this morning, though one of their horses collapsed and died of a heart attack at the end of the first chukka. Neither side wants this to happen, and Sikander admits that this is only one of several such deaths over the

---

[1] **avuncular**: caring
[2] **guile**: cleverness and cunning

last few years, grim reminders of the demands of such a physical game at such a high altitude.

He concedes that Gilgit's 'A' team are the favourites. They are unchanged from last year, and unlike Chitral's series of misfortunes, have had no casualties among their horses. I ask about the rumours I've heard about black magic and spells being put on the teams.

He shrugs.

'I never used to believe it, but now since everyone does, I've also started believing it.'

'You think it's more than just coincidence?'

He nods.

'More, yes, more than coincidence.'

He thinks the only possible advantage for Chitral is that they have Afghan horses, tough and strong after apprenticeships carrying men and goods over the high border passes. I ask what it will be like if they should lose tomorrow.

'Terrible. Terrible.'

He laughs, a little desperately.

'We try to go back in the dark. We pack up, get ready and leave at night.'

'Do they forgive quickly in Chitral?'

Sikander Ul-Mulk pauses, then shakes his head philosophically.

'It takes about a month or two.'

Day Eighteen

The weather is perfect.

A crowd, estimated at around 15,000, has gathered at the ground well in advance of the game. Apart from a VIP area on top of the main stand, the accommodation is basic, ranging from purpose-built concrete terraces to standing room on the various low mounds of glacial debris that enclose the playing area. One of these, with perhaps the least good view, is reserved for women.

The six players of each side parade onto the pitch, Chitral in scarlet, Gilgit in blue and white. Protection is optional. None of the Gilgit side wears protective headgear, whereas three of the Chitralis have helmets and one wears a *pakul*.

I'm squeezed into one of the terraces. There are no seats and we just settle ourselves as best we can on mud and stones. My eyes meet those of a policeman with riot helmet, night stick and dark glasses, sitting at the end of our row. He pulls on a cigarette and turns away. Above us is a line of brightly coloured kites, strung together, stretching right across the ground. (I later learn that there are 105 of them, thus winning, for a Doctor Ejazul Haq of Islamabad, the world record for the number of kites 'aired on a single thread'.)

Silence falls as a prayer is read out from the Koran. The horses canter forwards to the centre-line to receive the ball. Bulbul Jan, bareheaded, looks every bit the midfield general, effortlessly in control at the centre of his team.

202

Truc, less effortlessly in control, is the first to fertilize the pitch.

I don't blame him. If I was facing 50 minutes of constant running, sudden sprints, balls flying about and full-speed charges towards two-foot-high stone walls, I'd have probably done the same. In free-style polo the player is as much fair game as the ball and deliberate obstruction with either horse or mallet is a great skill. Nor are the horses and players the only ones taking risks. Mallets are dropped or broken with considerable frequency and stable boys take terrible risks rushing into the fray with replacements.

The game is non-stop, fast and even.

Predictably, Gilgit score first with Bulbul pushing in an easy goal after a furious build-up. He now gets to restart the game with a *tapokh*, which is very good to watch. The goal scorer races up the field at full gallop, holding both the ball and the mallet in the same hand, then, still with one hand only, releases the ball and strikes it ahead of him. It's often missed or half hit, but the apricot-wood hammer of Bulbul's stick meets the ball head on. It soars up the other end, bounces past the goal and is thrown back into play by a spectator, this keeping any interruption to the flow of play to a minimum. Maqbool pulls a goal back for Chitral and they go into the break unexpectedly level.

After a long interval display of ceremonial dancing, all hands and arms turning and twisting gracefully, the players are back on the pitch and a repeat of the first half is played out in the first few minutes. A Gilgit goal, then a

Chitral equalizer. As a well-informed spectator next to me says it's now all about the stamina of the horses.

Gilgit's powerful ponies begin to outrun Chitral, racing after the long ball with breathtaking speed. Two more Gilgit goals, then Bulbul Jan and the ageing Truc first set up a superb through pass for the fifth goal before running in the next one themselves. 6-2.

The Chitral supporters simply disappear at this point, streaming off the mounds and emptying the stands. Their departing cars send up columns of dust that blow over the ground as if bringing down a final curtain over their team's efforts.

The departure of these fair-weather supporters seems, perversely, to spur on the Chitral team and they pull back two goals in an unexpectedly nail-biting finish.

Gilgit have made it a hat trick of wins and won best player award. For Chitral there is the consolation of Best Horse, won by a tireless grey called Computer, and not much else but a night-time skulk back down the mountain.

I'm sure someone somewhere will claim it's been a victory for black magic.

Questions to apply to any literary non-fiction text

Before reading
1. What do I already know about this topic? What do I feel or think about it?
2. What is my purpose in reading this text? Do I have a specific task to do and if so, how will I need to approach it?
3. Who is the writer writing for? What are the clues that let me know?

During reading
4. How has the writer tried to hook me into the start of this text?
5. What ideas are introduced at the start of this text? How do I think the writer will develop them in the rest of the text?
6. What headline would I give to each paragraph to sum up its ideas?
7. What questions do I want to ask the author as I read this text?
8. What is striking about the way the writer uses language? Think about their vocabulary choices, the way that sentences are varied, the images created and any other special effects.

After reading
9. Now that I've read the whole text, how have my first ideas and responses changed?
10. What do I most remember about this text, and why?

11. Who would I recommend this text to? What are my reasons?
12. What makes this a successful example of literary non-fiction?

Acknowledgements

We are grateful to the following for permission to reproduce copyright material:

Granta Publications for an extract from *And When Did You Last See Your Father?* by Blake Morrison, and for an extract from *Mountains of the Mind* by Robert Macfarlane; The Random House Group Limited, for an extract from *Forgotten Voices of the Great War* by Max Arthur, published by Ebury Press; Victor Gollancz, a division of The Orion Publishing Group Limited, for an extract from *Toys Were Us* by Nicholas Whittaker, and for an extract from *Testament of Youth* by Vera Brittain; Liz Jobey for an extract from *Snaps* by Liz Jobey, published in *Granta Magazine*; Guardian Newspapers Limited for the articles 'The drowned world' by Tim Radford, published in *The Guardian* 11th September 2004, 'Williams hits new high as he delivers knockout blow to Iron Mike's career' by Kevin Mitchell, published in *The Observer* 1st August 2004, 'The race of her life: Holmes gets tactics right to seize gold' by Duncan Mackay, published in *The Observer*, 29th August 2004 and 'Fit for life?' by Diane Taylor, published in *The Guardian* 10th August 2004 © Guardian Newspapers Limited 2004; London Review of Books for an extract from 'Short Cuts' by Thomas Jones, published in *London Review of Books* 26.17 2nd September 2004 and for an extract from 'Hating Football' by Andrew O'Hagan, published in